About the Author

Dr. Ravi (Raveendra) Batra is a Professor of Economics at Southern Methodist University, Dallas, Texas. He has authored numerous articles on international economic problems in learned journals. Dr.Batra is regarded as one of the top trade theorists in the world. An article in *Economic Inquiry*, October 1978, included him among the five economist "superstars" in universities in America and Canada. Among his best known works are, *Studies in the Pure Theory of International Trade*, St. Martin's Press, *Theory of International Trade Under Uncertainty*, John Wiley & Sons, *Capitalism and Communism: A New Study of History*, Macmillan, and *Muslim Civilization and the Crisis in Iran*, Venus Books. He is the past associate-editor of the *Journal of International Economics* and the *Southern Economic Journal*.

To Sheila and Sunita

Success is the final step on the ladder of failure.

CONTENTS

Foreword

Analysts can basically be divided into two groups when it comes to explaining the course of human history. One group seeks explanations in cyclical regularities; the other seeks explanations in unique events or individuals. Both approaches have their strengths and weaknesses; both can be accused of biases. Those who believe in cyclical regularities are often justly accused of attempting to squeeze unique circumstances into their cyclical interpretations. Those who believe in unique events and individuals are often justly accused of ignoring broad social and economic forces that transcend unique individuals and events.

It is easy to see the appeal of both. If one could find cyclical regularities, the analyst could go beyond descriptions of the past and make predictions about the future. History would come alive as a predictive science. In terms of drama the unique event or person is much more exciting than cyclical regularities. Sudden unpredicted shocks and supermen combine to produce exciting results. Moreover future events seem to become more controllable. Future history is yet to be made by great individuals and is not dominated by uncontrollable social or economic forces.

It is also easy to see why the two approaches are usually at war with each other. To make its case each side has to argue that the other's prime explanations are of secondary importance. The 'great man' to the unique individual school of thought is neither 'great' nor 'unique' to the cyclical regularities and social forces school of thought. The 'cyclical regularities' seen by the analysts who believe in them are neither regular nor cyclical to those who believe in unique individuals or events. What are broad social forces to one become a stew of conflicting minor social forces to the other.

In reality history is obviously a combination of both elements. The two approaches are not mutually antithetical, and unique events or individuals can be the triggering mechanisms that explode broad social forces or set them off in new directions. For reasons that would probably take a psychiatrist to untangle it seems difficult for individual analysts, no matter how talented, to combine both approaches. Every analyst in practice tends to focus primarily on one or the other of the two major approaches.

Fortunately it is not necessary for any individual analyst to provide exactly the right judicious mixture of the two approaches. The reader gets that by understanding the explanations of both groups. History is too complicated and has too many facets for any one analyst or approach to reveal all of its complexities.

In seeking to explain inflation and depression Ravi Batra is an analyst of the cyclical school. He seeks to find broad economic or social forces rather than unique events or individuals to explain inflation and depression.

Depression is seen as a product of systematic tendencies for the distribution of wealth to become concentrated among a few. When this happens demand eventually sags relative to supply, and long cyclical down turns commence. Unlike some cyclical analysts Batra believes that such cycles are not inevitable and can be controlled with social policies essentially designed to stop undue concentrations of wealth from developing.

Essentially the economic problem is like that of the wolf and the caribou. If the wolves eat all of the caribou, the wolf also vanishes.Conversely if the wolves vanish, the caribou for a time multiply but eventually their numbers become too great and they die for lack of food. Producers need consumers and if producers deprive workers of their fair share of production income they essentially deprive themselves of the affluent consumers they need to make their facilities profitable. One could think of Batra's argument as a kind of economic ecology where there is a 'right' environmental balance.

Inflation is a more complicated problem since it can be seen as either cause or effect. Inflation and changes in the money supply go hand in hand, but which is the cause and which is the effect. The simplist model is one in which an independent decision maker (the government) increases the rate of growth of the money supply and creates inflation. From this perspective there is of course a simple solution. Mistaken policies of printing too much money should be replaced with policies that print less money. One only needs to ask why those directing the government printing presses are from time to time stupid.

In a more complicated model, inflation exogenously occurs (oil and food shocks might get it started for example), and governments print money to validate the inflation. To not print the money necessary to carry on transactions at the new higher price levels for oil and food would be to cause events, recessions because of falling demand for example, which governments are not prepared to tolerate. In this perspective the government technically could prevent inflation, but realistically it politically cannot.

In a still more complicated model the production of money itself is not under the control of the government. Whatever measure of money the government attempts to control, the market shifts to near substitutes and makes them into what is effectively money. Thus in August 1982 the American Federal Reserve Board announced that it was giving up on its attempts to control the American money supply on the grounds that new money market instruments were being invented so rapidly and in such large numbers that it could not effectively control the money supply Economic forces had essentially taken over the government's nominal role as printer of money.

Batra's problem is to sort out cause and effect in a money-inflation world where cause and effect is much more complicated than usually believed.

When it comes to the bottom line so beloved of economists, one can learn a lot about events by thinking about them in terms of cyclical regularities, of which Batra gives a novel and brilliant exposition, even if one believes that unique individuals and events are important.

March, 1985   Lester C. Thurow
                                      Gordon Y. Billard Professor
                                MIT, Cambridge, Massachusetts

PREFACE

This book sheds new and unconventional light on several controversial issues in macroeconomics, which, as is commonly recognized, is currently suffering from a great deal of confusion. Many different schools of macroeconomic thought, most of them at war with each other, exist today. Of these, Keynesian economics, Classical theory, and Monetarism are considered to be the main schools, and they offer dramatically different prescriptions.

This work provides a synthesis of the divergent views in macroeconomics. It reinterprets the historical record, going as far back as the 1750s, and demonstrates, once and for all, that money has been the primary determinant of economic activity in the United States. Monetarism thus stands vindicated at least in the American chronicle. Yet, Keynes' theory finds its proper place in the synthetic analysis provided in this work. It is argued that a point comes in the history of every decentralized, democratic society when a non-interventionist idea such as the Classical theory gives way to an interventionist philosophy such as Keynesian economics.

In writing this book, I have accumulated debt from many sources. I am grateful to my friend and former student, Thor Thorgeirsson, for invaluable moral support and useful discussion on this subject. Many other students in my classes, notably Kathleen Adler, Jamal Abu-Rashed, Sung-Sook Cho, Asif Dowla, Kishor Gharana, Hossein Gholami, Young-Kwang Lee, and Nadeem Naqvi, deserve credit for the clarification of my ideas.

I have also benefited a great deal from discussions with my colleagues, Professors W.R. Russell, Thomas Fomby, Phil Porter, Daniel Slottje, and Josef Hadar. Speedy and accurate typing by Elizabeth Jenkins-Smith, Ruth Henderson, Debbie Skrakowski, Susan Meyn and Lynda Morrison is responsible for the timely appearance of this work. Finally Sunita Chaudhary helped me in drawing charts and diagrams.

Dallas, Texas   Ravi Batra

February, 1985

1
Overview

This book is a study of cycles—cycles of a kind unheard of before. Its focus is on fluctuations in various socio-economic variables. Most ideas reflect needs of the times, and economic theory is no exception. During the depression decade of the 1930s, economists chiefly sought to explain the deep quagmire that had trapped the system for so long. Some scholars explored short-term fluctuations, while others attempted to unravel the long-term waves in business activity. During the relatively stable decades of the fifties and sixties, experts turned mainly to esoteric mathematical models designed to refine, and in some cases reformulate, the long-established theories in economics. Gone was the concern about cycles—short and long. The business cycle came to be regarded as obsolete.

However, the 1970s witnessed two major recessions, and with them the old interest in cycles made a comeback. But this time, problems were far more complex than before, for the recessions were unexpectedly accompanied by persistent inflation. Orthodox theories and conjectures about economic oscillations were not equal to the new challenge. So many forecasts, based on outmoded ideas, proved wrong that at times the economist's sermons invited open skepticism from the public. Today, it is widely recognized that the puzzle of business cycles, despite myriad attempts to solve it, has so far eluded the economic profession.

All the cycles discovered thus far have displayed varying periodicity. The economic literature speaks of a Mitchel cycle which is forty to fifty months long, a Jugular cycle varying from nine to eleven years, a Kuznets-type intermediate cycle of fifteen to twenty-five years, and finally a Kondratieff long-wave cycle lasting anywhere from forty to sixty years. All these are irregular cycles.

The cycles reported in the present work, however, belong to a different genus. They may be called regular or rhythmical cycles, because they display an exact periodicity. Besides, some of them deal with variables commonly regarded as exogenous in economic theory. Money supply, for instance, is a case in point. It is supposed to be determined by the Federal Reserve System. But it turns out to have had a rhythmical cycle, which can be traced as far back as the birth of the American nation.

The book reports exact patterns in four economic variables, namely money supply, inflation, regulation, and depressions, and explains them with the help of a socio-economic and historical theory called the law of social cycle. The time-path of these variables has been so exact for so long that they easily lead to reliable forecasts—both short and long. In fact, it is this type of historical analysis that in the past has enabled me to make a wide variety of bold predictions.

On December 5, 1978, in a lecture at the University of Oklahoma at Norman, responding to questions raised by an audience of three hundred students and professors, I made the following statements:

1.   The Shah of Iran would be overthrown in a revolution in 1979, and the clergy would take over the reins of government.

2.   In 1980-81 Iran and Iraq would start a bloody war, which would continue for seven years, and by 1986 the entire Moslem world in the Middle East would be caught in this conflict.

3. Europe would experience a depression in 1986-87.

4. The depression would spread to America by 1989-90 and then turn into an all-time economic disaster plaguing the whole world.

5. Capitalism would be overhauled in the 1990s and so would Communism at the turn of the century, culminating in a global golden age.

Subsequently the gist of my lecture appeared in two Nashville newspapers that interviewed me just after the Iran-Iraq war which began in earnest in September 1980. (See references [18 and 31] at the end of the book).

By now it is evident that the first two of my predictions, all politely ridiculed in 1978, have come true with some accuracy. The Shah of Iran abdicated in January, 1979 and the Moslem priesthood, headed by Ayatollah Khomeini, came to power in February of the same year. Similarly, the Iran-Iraq conflict, already in its fourth year, began in September 1980 and still shows no sign of ending. I am confident that my other predictions will follow in due course.

How is it that I was able to foresee the upheaval in the Middle East with accuracy? What makes me think that the world is going to face momentous changes in the near future? I am no astrologer, no psychic, not even an expert palmist. But I am an economist and a student of history and the economist has a birthright to make forecasts, even if they have proved grossly inaccurate in recent years.

I have earlier explained the analysis underlying the first two predictions. (See [3]). The present book examines the reasoning on which the other three conclusions are based. It also explores what an average person can do today to survive the catastrophe of the 1990s; how he should prepare himself while there is still some time.

The conclusions reached in this book derive from a diagnosis of history and economic theory. My interest in history began in earnest in 1976 when I chanced to read an analysis of society by P.R. Sarkar, a leading scholar from India, who has profoundly enriched the literature in several areas including economics, political science, poetry, psychology, linguistics, art and, above all, spirituality. As I went through Sarkar's *Human Society* [26], I was awe-struck by the generality and depth of his vision. Here finally was an answer to the puzzle of social evolution; here finally was a philosophy of history that in one stroke could unravel the mystery of every social phenomenon. In one profound doctrine, Sarkar had assimilated the ideas of all past historiographers.

The next chapter examines in detail what Sarkar calls the law of social cycle. Here I simply speak of the process that led me to my rather farfetched predictions about the future course of existing societies. As I grasped the law of social cycle, which claimed universal application, I decided to see for myself if indeed it had been upheld by the chronicle of various civilizations. I labored through the history of four different societies—Egyptian, Western, Russian and Indo-Aryan—and concluded that each one of them had indeed evolved in tune with the pattern described by Sarkar's philosophy. My inquiry into the human past had by then become all but obsessive. A by product of that obsession was my work on world history, a book that was completed towards the end of 1977 and published the next year. [1].

The book explained the theory of social cycle, argued that it was more general than the views of Marx and Toynbee combined, and then demonstrated that the chronicles of four societies mentioned above fitted precisely into Sarkar's pattern.

The centerpiece of a philosophy of history is an idea called historical determinism, meaning that history follows a certain pattern, which is observable and which can be used to forecast the future course of events. That is precisely what my book did. It first showed that the four civilizations had indeed evolved along the social cycle expounded by Sarkar, and then went on to predict the future of Western, Russian and Indo-Aryan societies. The predictions indicated turmoil, upheaval and revolutions by the year 2000, unless something was done in time.

In 1978, after completing the book, I turned to the study of other civilizations, notably the Chinese and the Moslem. I am an economist by training and profession, and specialize in building esoteric but unrealistic mathematical models of international trade. The word had gotten around about my sudden foray into history and about the unusual nature of my conclusions. In November 1978, I received an invitation from Dr. Eden Yu of the economics department and from Mr. Muhammad Waziri, then the secretary of Omicorn Delta Epsilon, to visit the University of Oklahoma and give two lectures. They insisted that, among other things, I speak on the future of capitalism and communism. So it was that on the 5th of December, I found myself facing a large audience of students and professors at Norman.

When I wrote my first book on history, my ideas were still in the formative stage. I had a general view of the future of various societies, but the specifics still eluded me. Even where I felt that such and such event would occur in a particular year, I lacked the confidence to put it in writing. I had some proof, but not sufficient proof.

Shortly after the publication of my work in 1978, Iran experienced an eruption—with a bang. I had expected this all along, but lacked conviction to include it in my book. By August 1978, the Iranian turmoil was in full swing. There were daily protests and demonstrations by the public matched by police shootings and brutality. The anticipated tumult in Iran, with all its ramifications, is one spark that I needed to shed my customary caution and declare openly the exact years during which I expected certain events to occur. This I did at the first opportunity that arose during my lecture at Norman, and boldly made my five predictions mentioned before.

As stated earlier, I have already explained the reasoning underlying my first two predictions in a work published in 1980. Since then I have gathered new data about the American economy, and now feel that I can prove to others what I have believed and taught my students for so many years. At this time my arguments find support not only from the law of social cycle but also from a variety of statistics. I am convinced more than ever before that an unprecedented depression will afflict the American and the world economy in 1989-90 and last for seven years.

The present work combines the arguments that I have previously presented in two books on history with my current research that the dominant variables in U.S. economy have moved along an exact cycle of three decades. Specifically, I have discovered that, except during the trauma following the American Civil War of 1860s, the rate of inflation has reached its peak *every third decade* over the past two centuries. Simultaneously, the rate of growth of money has also crested *every third decade* over the same time period. Another variable displaying an identical pattern is the degree of government regulation of the economy. In other words, the peak decades of inflation and money growth also turn out to be the peak decades of government regulation.

These are amazing and incredible features of the American society. They verge on the miraculous and have never been discovered before. Ignoring the two decades immediately following the Civil War, we find that U.S. economy has moved along virtually a pre-destined path ever since Independence. Regardless of the massive socio-economic transformations dotting the republic, inflation, money growth and the government regulation of business have crested together every third decade. It is as if a supernatural power has been dictating the evolutionary course of the American economic system.

As regards economic contractions, the three-decade pattern described above still holds, but with a modification. A steep recession has occurred every decade since the 1780s. A depression, which is far worse than a recession, occurred every third or sixth decade, in the sense that if the third decade experienced only a recession, then the sixth decade witnessed an all-time disaster.

What will cause the depression of the 1990s? The book argues that the same forces that precipitated the disaster of the 1930s are at work today. In addition, U.S. and world economies are currently burdened by a heavy load of debt, which did not exist in the 1930s and which is likely to make things much worse in the near future.

Economists generally blame the cataclysm of the 30s on faulty monetary and fiscal policies of the government. This book contends that the primary cause of that depression, or of any other, has so far eluded the experts. There was nothing new in the monetary and fiscal policies of those times. The government had followed similar policies during previous recessions also. What was so different that turned an ordinary recession of 1930 into an unprecedented collapse? The answer lies in the unprecedented concentration of wealth that peaked in 1929. This concentration is again rising today (1984) and beginning to assume menacing levels of the 1920s.

The analysis is organized as follows: Chapter 2 examines Sarkar's law of social cycle, whereas Chapters 3, 4 and 5 focus on the long-run cycles of money growth, inflation and regulation in the United States. These cycles have followed exactly the same pattern by jointly cresting every third decade, except during the immediate aftermath of the Civil War, *when they are all disrupted alike.* Chapter 6 attempts to read the pattern underlying the steep recessions and depressions that have periodically convulsed the economic and social fiber. This pattern is not as clear-cut as that discernible in earlier chapters. But exist it does.

Chapter 7 weaves various threads of the previous chapters to argue that the depression of the 1990s is now all but inevitable, whereas Chapter 8 explores what an average person could do today to prepare for the crisis now in the making. Chapter 9 prescribes certain reforms that could be currently followed to possibly keep the economy form lapsing into the depression. Chapter 10 furnishes a general theory of inflation. Finally, Chapter 11 provides a synthesis of the divergent schools of macroeconomics in terms of the all-comprehensive law of social cycle.

2

Sarkar's Law
of Social Cycle

How society evolves is a question that has baffled many minds since ancient times. Plato, Aristotle, St. Augustine, Marx, Spengler, Toynbee, among others, have tried to solve this puzzle, but their ideas, once the cause of much intellectual ferment, have been either discarded or considered seriously lacking. It is not that they have been forgotten, for in their thought there is much that will endure forever, only that few today concede their claims of universality. Their method of analysis, namely the method of historical determinism wherein the student attempts to detect a pattern in the maze of historical events, is an idea that has long been regarded as dead.

However, Prabhat Ranjan Sarkar, a philosopher of profound learning, has recently resurrected this idea in terms of a theory called the law of social cycle. Many scholars have endeavored to discern in the chaos of history a certain rhythm, an imperceptible harmony complying with natural laws, but their peers, suspicious of any theorizing about the seemingly arbitrary social phenomenon, have scoffed at their views. Sarkar's contribution, however, belongs to a different genus. It is immune at least to those strictures to which other philosophies of history have been subjected.

Historical Determinism

One reason the idea of historical determinism has traditionally invited so much hostility is its popular misconception. True, the concept definitely means that history follows a set pattern; that society evolves and undergoes transformations in tune with a discernible rhythm. But it does not imply, as is commonly believed, that man cannot make his own destiny; nor does it signify fatalism and resignation before the might of Providence.

All historical determinism means is that, while man indeed is the architect of his own fate, he has to operate within bounds determined by a higher principle—Nature. While natural laws cannot be defied, we can work within their perimeter to generate a better environment—a better society. Certainly, water by its nature flows downward. This law can never be reversed no matter how hard we try. But does it mean that the life-giving river flowing down the hills to the plains cannot be tamed and harnessed to our advantage? Thus all historical determinism means is that the arena within which man is free to play is already predetermined by the principle of social evolution. And it is this arena that Sarkar sets out to explain. To him society is a dynamic entity, relentlessly moving, never at rest.

While man is free to decide his own course of action, he faces limits imposed by society in which he lives. He can determine his own evolution but not social evolution which, in the interest of order in the world, must follow dictates of Nature.

The Four Social Classes

Sarkar begins with general characteristics of the human mind. He argues that even though most people have common goals and ambitions, their methods of achieving their objectives may differ from person to person, depending on inner qualities of the individual. Most of us, for instance, seek living comforts and social prestige. But some of us try to attain them by developing intellectual skills, some by developing physical skills, and some by accumulating wealth. Finally, some people have little ambition in life and they form a class by themselves. Thus, according to Sarkar society is basically composed of four types of people, each endowed with a different frame of mind.

People have common objectives, but their *modus operandi* to attain them differ because of sharp differences in their innate abilities and qualities. Some persons, born with great physique and bodily strength, excel in physical skills requiring stamina, courage and vigor. Such people are usually employed in occupations involving physical risks. Sarkar calls them persons of warrior mentality. In his view, soldiers, policemen, fire fighters, professional athletes, skilled blue-collar workers, etc., belong to the class of warriors in the sense that all these occupations require physical strength and skills. Thus, anyone who tries to solve his problems with the help of his might and muscle belongs to the class of warriors or has a warrior-like mind.

There is another type of person who lacks the physical energy of the warrior but is endowed with relatively superior intellect. Being so endowed, he or she tries to develop mental skills to do well in society. To Sarkar, everyone attempting to solve his problems with the help of his brains rather than brawn is an intellectual. This is a much broader concept than is generally believed. But Sarkar's usage of the term is all-comprehensive. To him, not just professors, writers and scholars, but even lawyers, physicians, poets, scribes, engineers, scientists, white-collar workers, and, above all, priests are intellectuals because they all utilize their keen mind rather than muscle power to attain their goals.

There is yet another type of person who, according to Sarkar, tends to accumulate wealth to achieve what is generally regarded as the good life. Such people are also bright, but their mind runs mainly after money. They are smarter than the warrior-type but not as intelligent as the intellectual. Yet they are usually more affluent than the other two. Sarkar calls such people acquisitors, because virtually all their propensities are engaged in amassing wealth. To them money is all that matters in life; opulence alone is their key to success and prosperity. Merchants, bankers, money lenders, capitalists, businessmen, landlords generally belong to the class of acquisitors. While other classes seek wealth to enjoy material goods, the acquisitor covets money for the sake of money.

Finally, there is a fourth type of person who is altogether different from the other three. He is the unskilled worker or the physical laborer. He lacks the vigor of the warrior, the brilliance of the intellectual and the accumulating instinct of the acquisitor. He is also wanting in the high ambition of the other three. His education is relatively low and he is usually deficient in marketable skills. For all these handicaps, the unskilled worker is, and has always been, exploited by the rest of society. He does the work deemed dirty by others, yet he is the poorest among all classes. Peasants, serfs, unskilled factory workers generally belong to the class of physical laborers.

Exceptions, of course, may be found among those engaged in unskilled occupations. Some peasants or farm workers may be persons of keen intelligence, or there may be other workers who perform hard labor not by choice but under social coercion. Such persons do not belong to the laboring class. Similarly, in virtually all societies in the past slavery was common, and slaves were forced to do the servile, physical work. In no way does it mean that the slaves belonged to the class of unskilled workers. The laboring class is simply composed of people who perform physical labor by choice, or because they are unable to acquire technical skills. Even though possessing some bodily strength, they lack the initiative, ambition and drive to succeed in the world: seldom do they shine in society.

These then are the four classes which exist in every society and have existed since ancient times. Sarkar calls it the quadri-divisional social system. He differs sharply from Marx and other socialists who define classes on economic grounds—on the basis of income and wealth. Sarkar, of course, does not neglect the economic aspect, but to him it is only one of the four aspects describing the totality of society. Class divisions, in his view, persist because of inherent differences in human nature.

It is worth pointing out that Sarkar's division of society into four groups is quite flexible, especially over the long run. Social mobility among the groups may occur if an individual's mentality changes over time. Through concerted effort, or through prolonged contact with others, a person may move into the realm of the other class. For example, a laborer, under long army drills and training, may become an accomplished warrior, or through diligence and vigorous education he or she may become an intellectual, and so on. Similarly, the intellectual, under the influence of money, may turn into an acquisitor, or an acquisitor into a laborer. Thus even though class distinctions in society derive from innate differences in human endowments and nature, they may or may not be hereditary.

Yet the possibility of social mobility should not be exaggerated. Although, it is possible for a person to acquire skills of the other type, it is not easy. A boxer, for instance, will find it hard to become a scientist, and vice versa. An acquisitor will also have the same problem. He will have a tough time becoming a warrior or an intellectual. But the point is that it is not impossible.

Wherever civilization developed, in Africa, Asia, Europe and elsewhere, a careful examination of history reveals the existence of the four-pronged division of society sketched by Sarkar. His categories of mind are comprehensive enough to cover the full range of a mature society. Thus every civilization, which is what a mature society is, consists of four sections, each comprising people reflecting the predominance of a certain type of mind. Ordinarily, individual behavior displays two, or even all, of the four attitudes, but for the most part and especially under duress, only one mental tendency betrays its true colors. There is a bit of acquisitive instinct in most of us, but only a few constantly long for money and make it the *summum bonum* of their life. We are all after a comfortable living standard and social prestige, but some of us attain them by means of physical force and skills, some through intellectual pursuits and excellence, and some by ceaselessly saving money or making more money with money already at hand. In this order, we are warriors, intellectuals and acquisitors. Those of us imbued with little ambition or drive, wanting in basic education and skills of the time, are the physical workers.

In every society, warriors maintain law and order, intellectuals supply theories and religion, acquisitors are adept at managing the economy and laborers do the unskilled jobs.

The Law of Social Cycle

Having described the four types of people in society, I am now in a position to present the law of social cycle. In accordance with his quadri-divisional social system, Sarkar argues that a society evolves over time in terms of four distinct eras. Sometime warriors, sometime intellectuals and sometime acquisitors dominate the social and political scene. Laborers never hold the reins, but at times the ruling class becomes so self-centered and corrupt that for a while a large majority of people is reduced to poverty. The general public, engaged mostly in making a living, has then little time left for the finer aspects of life—art, music, adventure, poetry, spirituality. Such a time may be called the age of laborers.

No single group can exercise social supremacy and power forever. What is more interesting, as well as intriguing, is that the movement of society from one epoch to another follows a definite pattern. Specifically, in the development of every civilization, ancient or modern, oriental or occidental,

> the era of laborers is followed by the era of warriors, the era of warriors by the era of intellectuals, and the era of intellectuals by the era of acquisitors, culminating in a social revolution—such a social evolution is the infallible Law of Nature. [26, p. 40].

This is Sarkar's law of social cycle. Note the word evolution. This law of nature is "infallible", because it is based on the evolutionary principle. Just as human evolution is indisputable, just as the onward march of humanity cannot be arrested, so is the movement of social cycle an inevitable natural phenomenon, where social hegemony shifts from one class to another, from the collectivity of one type of mind to another. Thus underneath the seemingly haphazard change in society lies the invisible but unmistakable imprint of Mother Nature. Social evolution goes hand in hand with human evolution.

It is in such apocalyptic terms that Sarkar conveys his message. To him society is a dynamic entity and perpetual change is its essence. A civilization emerges with the rise of warriors, and after considerable ups and downs through the era of intellectuals, acquisitors and laborers, it goes back to the warrior age, only to resume its evolutionary march in tune with the same old rhythm. This, in short, is Sarkar's social cycle.

Era of Laborers

How do we recognize the era of laborers? The laboring

society is one that suffers from a complete lack of guidance, leadership and authority; one where the so-called leaders become so egocentric and greedy that the majority of people, following in their footsteps, display "laboring mentality," a mentality ruled by instinctive behavior, greed and pure self-concern. The era of laborers is then characterized by near anarchy, by a lack of social order. There the family ties are not binding, people laugh at higher values and finer things of life, morals are extremely loose, crime is rampant, and materialism permeates society to the core. All laborer societies in ancient times were primitive, and remained primitive until some warriors emerged and wrested leadership in their own hands.

What distinguishes a civilization from a primitive community has for some time been a matter of controversy among historians. Sarkar's division of society into four classes in accordance with their mental characteristics, however, suggests a straightforward definition. Using his concepts, a primitive society is one where all its members display laboring mentality, so that it has little chance of growing out of the chasm of ignorance and savage existence. The rise of civilizations may then be ascribed to the rise of persons with non-laboring mentality, especially those endowed with warriorlike qualities.

One way to differentiate between workmen and other groups is to look at their level of education. In general, the schooling is the highest among intellectuals and the lowest among the unskilled, with warriors and acquisitors standing somewhere in the middle. In many societies in the past, only priests had the ability to read and write. The access to education was then considered a privilege of which the laboring peasants, serfs and unskilled workers were totally deprived. Today educational facilities are available to all, yet physical laborers are relatively the least educated. The schooling of warriors and acquisitors is difficult to compare, but the intellectuals clearly excel other groups in this regard.

Of one issue there is little doubt. The early history of humankind, the pre-historic or the Paleolithic period —covering the times of *Homo habilis* to the Java man, to the Neanderthal man and finally to our immediate ancestor, the Cro-Magnon man—belongs to the laboring era, which may be traced back to 1,750,000 B.C. when the Paleolithic men are supposed to have evolved enough from apes to perform what archaeologists and historians call astonishing feats. There is some evidence that the Neanderthal and Cro-Magnon men, who lived in caves, had begun to cook their food and bury their dead. Group life, which is traceable to the lower Paleolithic culture, had become more regular and organized with the advent of Cro-Magnon men. Their supermost achievement, however, is in art (especially painting) which throws ample light on what is known as the upper Paleolithic culture.

Although group life had been established during the Paleolithic age, the essentials of an organized society were still absent. The institution of marriage and family life were yet to evolve. Men and women lived together not in a morally and legally binding relationship, but purely because of biological attraction to each other. They felt little love for their own children, much less for their fellow beings. Each powerful man had several concubines: being feebler than men, women had to accept an inferior status. Since there was no government, there was no law and order; there was anarchy, with everyone preoccupied with self-preservation.

Today, over the eons, we have all evolved to an extent that our relapse to the prehistoric culture, to that savage existence, is inconceivable. Can we then say that humanity cannot now degenerate into the laborer era? The answer is no.

Everything in this world is relative, changing with respect to time and place. A laborer society today would be similar in some respects to its counterpart in ancient times, but it cannot exactly be the same; that would be

17

negating the fruit of millions of years of natural evolution. The laborer's mind is now much more intelligent than it was at the birth of human consciousness; no longer need it be passive in the absolute sense. A laborer today is one with low initiative and drive relative to the other types of people. And for this reason, in all countries the laboring class is exploited as much today as in the past. Its toil is still indispensable to the survival of any society, but ruling classes are taking advantage of it everywhere in the world.

The distinctive feature of a laborer society today would be the open disregard of governmental authority and law by its dominant members. Thus, unlike the Paleolithic age, government may exist in contemporary laborer society, but its command would not be respected; violent crime would become rampant, with people living in fear. In ancient times there were no family ties worth the name. Today, by the same token, the weakening of family bonds would be reflected in the indiscipline of children and their disrespect for parental authority, in frequent divorces and other marital violence, and in the heartless removal of the elderly from the family. Women had a lowly status in the distant past; in today's laborer society, such inferiority would be manifested in high prostitution, pornography as well as the general exploitation of women by men.

In short, if all, or most, of these characteristics prevail in a society, it is unmistakably languishing through the laborer age. A close scrutiny of history reveals that all civilizations, including those now alive, occasionally had to pass through the pangs of such periods. There were times when they were shaken by internal fissures or external assaults. Actually the difference between the extinct and existing civilizations is simply that some societies were crushed by the laboring times, whereas others came out of them to resume their forward march of evolution.

The Warrior Era

The era of warriors, in terms of the political and social structure, is diametrically opposite to the era of laborers. In the military age, the army headed by a dictator—King, Emperor, President—controls the government as well as society. There the political authority is extremely centralized in the form of an absolute government, people are highly disciplined, family ties are morally binding, women are well-respected and so on. Intellectuals and acquisitors enjoy some respect in the military age, although they have little say in governance. But laborers perform the physical labor for the warrior and in the closing stage of this period, as in that of every other era, they are mercilessly exploited. However, at the dawn of the warrior age, the ruler respects their contribution and treats them with care and compassion. Laborers, though physically strong, lack the enterprising and adventurous spirit of the warriors, who use their physical skills to advance in life, to excel within their circle. It is this spirit that enabled Columbus to discover America, Robert Peary to reach the North Pole, Edmund Hillary and Ten Zing to climb Mount Everest. Propelled by the same spirit, the Russians launched a Sputnik and the Americans set their footprints on the moon.

A warrior believes in physical discipline, in firm authority over his family, and when he comes to power, his family extends to the entire people living in his domain. Therefore a warrior ruler believes in authoritarian government, in absolutism. That is why military eras have always been characterized by political centralization, by the divine right of kings, monarchs and dictators.

Going back to ancient times, it may be seen that the warrior era began with the Neolithic period or the New Stone Age, which seems to have been established by 3000 B.C., although in Egypt it had emerged by as early as 5000 B.C. The Neolithic age is marked by the beginning of agriculture and the domestication of animals. This is the period when men and women began to live out of caves to attain a better mastery over the environment than their forefathers. What else but an adventurous spirit could have inspired them to go out and look for dependable sources of food? In the words of Burns and Ralph, "whereas all the men who had lived heretofore were mere food-gatherers, Neolithic man was a food-producer." [8, p. 13].

Another distinct feature of this period is the rise of institutions, for which a highly organized group and social life is essential. The origin of state may also be ascribed to this period, where the discovery of agriculture and the subsequent population explosion made social organization indispensable to survival.

Although traces of Neolithic culture can be observed in places even today, it is supposed to have ended when metal was discovered. In Egypt it terminated as early as 4000 B.C., and in Europe by 2000 B.C.[1]. In most other parts of the world, such as the Middle East and Persia, where primitive societies were replaced by ancient civilizations, the Neolithic age came to an end around 3000 B.C. However, the military era seems to have continued with few interruptions, although, in accordance with general human evolution, it underwent drastic changes. In order to distinguish the earliest warrior epoch of a society from the later ones, a distinction important to ancient civilizations, the Neolithic period may be called the tribal warrior age.

In the immediate post-Neolithic age, the military era is represented by the supremacy of royalties—kings, emperors, monarchs, dictators. The ancient Egypt, the Rig-Vedic age in India, ancient Greece, ancient Rome, and ancient Persia are prime examples of societies where a distinction needs to be made between the tribal and the subsequent imperial warrior age.

In the military age, the sense of discipline, first in the family and then in society, is extremely strong and for this reason women enjoy a high social status, at least higher than their stature in other eras. In the Neolithic period, many different tribes were led by great fighters. Being constantly at war with each other, they soon discovered the importance of numerical strength. Fast growth of population thus became their common objective, an objective in which women were at least equal partners. On this account, and to maintain the purity of blood, brave and daring women were honored as Group Mothers in Neolithic times. Thus the early warrior society was governed by a matriarch who provided lineal identity to every man and woman belonging to a particular clan.

The institution of marriage first emerged in the tribal warrior age. In the laborer era there was hardly any marital life. Men and women lived together purely because of biological needs. Consequently children did not know who their father was, but everyone knew who the mother was. This is another reason why women enjoyed greater respect than men in those times. That is why when civilization first sprouted from the soil of primitive society, brave and energetic women became the leaders as Group Mothers. This is how various tribes were born, most headed by a woman.

Once society was organized into tribes, men and women began to feel a certain sense of bond in their conjugal relations. At the same time, the father came to have a sense of duty and responsibility towards his offspring. Consequently, woman's burden in raising children declined to an extent, and with this began the decline in her social status as well. Gradually families began to be dominated by men who were also the bread-winners. In time, Matriarchy gave way to Patriarchy wherein the tribal head was a man, and in which descent was recognized in his name. How long the Group Mothers dominated society cannot be easily ascertained, but it appears that Patriarchy had emerged before the end of Neolithic times. As woman's influence declined, men began to have many wives towards the close of the tribal age.

During Paleolithic days also, there were frequent fights among the people, but they were initiated solely by self-preservation. In the warrior era, however, the army officers and their soldiers recruited from the ranks of laborers, warred for their own survival as well as that of others. Whereas workmen had fought for food and shelter, warriors fought for dignity and self-esteem as well. In due time, however, the military rulers became highly authoritarian; they lost much of their early benevolence, and as a result the soldiers and laborers were mercilessly exploited. Their domains also expanded manifold; many tribes were unified after lengthy warfare into vast kingdoms headed by monarchs and emperors. In the holocausts that the militarists unleashed on each other, laborers were the helpless participants. And for what? For the momentary ego gratification of the megalomaniac warrior who craved supremacy over the entire world. In most militaristic societies, the bloody wars of conquests portended the end of army domination and the birth of the era of intellectuals, who, represented by the priesthood or prime ministers, came to power in every civilization at the end of the military age.

Era of Intellectuals

Despotic governments of the militarists were fundamentally unstable, for nothing based on fire and sword can command obedience from the people for long. The absolute rulers had felt the need for theories that could justify their arbitrary rule. In this they were ably assisted by those endowed with a keen wit—the intellectuals. To pursue their careers, the scholars volunteered theories that justified the ruler's absolute authority over his people. Thus were born such concepts as the infallibility of monarchs and the divine right of kings. That is why, in the heyday of the military age the intellectuals enjoyed a social status second only to warriors. Therefore when the army influence declined as a result of sanguinary wars, the power-and-leadership vacuum could be filled only by men of knowledge who alone commanded enough respect and authority at the time. Everywhere do we find that intellectuals came to power in the aftermath of the bloodshed caused by warfare. In the West, for instance, the Catholic Church rose to primacy after the fall of the militaristic Roman empire.

The intellectual's mind is one that lacks the gallantry of the warrior but abounds in foresight and keenness of intellect. In general a scholar is cautious and pragmatic; he or she relishes comfort but not the physical labor that it requires. Actually his physique is not built for this purpose. Consequently, the intellectuals attain power only by defeating the warrior in the battle of wits. They rule indirectly—through their control over the apparent warrior ruler who alone has the physical and mental aptitude to keep order in society. Whenever, and wherever, the intellectuals perceived that the time for their rule had come, they devised new cults and dogmas rationalizing their hold on the people. First they managed to convince the warrior of the possibility of his perdition after death, and then concocted rituals so complex that the latter earnestly sought their religious service. This the intellectuals were more than glad to provide in exchange for political power and creature comforts.

After outwitting the warrior, the intellectuals set out to inject baseless fears and prejudices in other classes as well. Once the apparent ruler was won over, it was just a matter of time before the rest of society yielded to their self-serving doctrines. Thus we find that in every civilization the general public was once caught in the stranglehold of theories by priests, theologians and other scholars.

The structure of government and administrative machinery in the era of intellectuals changes little from that prevailing in the military age, except that now, because of the weakness of the apparent ruler, the real authority is exercised by someone behind the scenes. Yet the scholars need the warriors to maintain their control over the general public, and, therefore, the government is now somewhat decentralized: The apparent ruler is no longer absolute, nor is the indirect ruler.

The early warrior period, as noted before, was marked by Matriarchy, a social order in which Group-Mothers had dominated; this was followed by Patriarchy in which the male head of the tribe became supreme; and finally came the absolute monarchs and emperors. Due to the warrior's innate magnanimity, woman continued to enjoy high respect in society. Throughout the tribal era she was regarded as man's co-helper, commanding sufficient, if not equal, social prestige.

In the era of intellectuals, however, woman came to be regarded as inherently inferior to man. In the militaristic era, at least in its first half, the warrior's manliness enabled him to treat woman, despite her physical weakness, on a more or less equal footing with man. An intellectual, however, lacks the warrior's courage, and consequently is always afraid of insubordination by other groups. He has to be, lest the muscular warriors and laborers see through his shaky dogmas and cast him aside. Thus a scholar, in order to rule, will always try to subjugate other groups, much less allow them equal rights.

After besting the warrior in the intellectual arena, the male scholars proceeded to bind women as well in the web of theories; and in this case, the web was even tighter than that binding men. Women were denied access to scriptures as well as education in many countries. At some places their subservience to men came close to slavery, whereas at others they were slighted as housewives. The husband was, and in places is, considered God Almighty to his wife. Today, we find it hard to believe that even in the West, which had supposedly shaken off dogmatic irrationalism after the Middle Ages, women were deprived of voting rights as late as the 20th century.

True, women have by now come a long way in attaining freedom, but the idea of woman as inherently inferior, as a property, as a plaything of men persists in many parts of the world. Woman's humiliation, however, began only with the intellectual's era, and if it has endured so long the blame rests squarely with men of letters. In line with the general double-talk of such men, in theory woman was accorded a status equal to man. She was called better-half or fair sex, but in practice the essence of such labels was openly flouted.

The era of intellectuals scored another first when prostitution came into being. In the laborer as well as warrior times, especially towards the end of the military age when men had many wives, some lechery did exist in society. Warriors even went to war over women, but prostitution as an institution had not yet been born. Credit for its birth goes solely to the priests who made women totally dependent on men. Without a husband, woman economically became a cripple; prostitution presumably began when widows or other women could not find husbands, and there was no other recourse. More important, however, were the priestly coaxing and pressures on virgins to dedicate themselves to the service of temple gods. This is how the so called temple prostitution developed in ancient communities of Egypt, Greece and India among others. In Lacroix's vivid words:

> As soon as religions had been born from the fear
> inspired in the heart of man by sight of the great
> commotions of nature, as soon as the volcano, the
> tempest, the thunderbolt, the earthquake and
> the angry sea had led him to invent gods,
> prostitution offered herself to those same
> terrible and implacable deities, and the priest
> took for himself an offering from which the gods
> represented would have been unable to profit.

> . . . .Prostitution became, from then on, the
> essence of certain cults of gods and goddesses
> who ordained, tolerated or encouraged it. Hence
> sprang the mysteries of Lampascus, of Babylon,
> of Paphos and of Memphis; hence the infamous
> traffic which was carried on at the gates of
> temples; hence those monstrous idols with which
> the virgins of India prostituted themselves;
> hence the obscene dictatorship which the priests
> arrogated to themselves under the auspices of
> their impure divinities. [20 pp. 6-7].

Era of Acquisitors

Nothing irrational or illogical can endure forever. The
web in which the literary men had caught the rest of society
began to loosen as other sections slowly saw through their
theories. Quite fittingly, and perhaps ironically, some
elements within the intellectual class itself began to
question the priest's intentions. Not only the elaborate
rituals but also the luxury and lifestyle of the priesthood
came under fire. Among the scholars themselves there had
occurred a good deal of argumentation and doctrinal
battles, and those who were thus defeated started
accumulating wealth to compensate for their intellectual
debility. Similarly, some warriors also followed that route.
In this way, another mentality evolved in human beings;
another class, one obsessed with money—the "acquisitive"
mind.

In the meanwhile, all forms of authoritarianism
—monarchic as well as ecclesiastic—had been challenged
by certain intellectual reformers. New philosophies of
individualism, as opposed to state collectivism, were
gradually sinking in public consciousness. Philosophical
pillars of the doctrine of divine right of kings as well as of
churchmen had been fatally undermined. As a result of all
these developments, the power base slowly drifted towards

the wealthy class of acquisitors: thus began the acquisitive age.

In all civilizations, the acquisitive class consisted of the rich belonging to such diverse groups as landlords, capitalists, money lenders and merchants. No longer was it enough to have a keen intellect to attain comforts and political power. Instead, social prominence passed into the hands of the wealthy.

An acquisitor differs from an intellectual mainly in the way each uses his intellect. The latter, while interested in comfortable living and material acquisition, is inclined to literary pursuits for their own sake; he likes theorizing about any phenomenon. However, the acquisitive mind would have none of this; its intellect is obsessed with amassing, not just enjoying, wealth. It is this acquisitive mentality that reigns during the age of the wealthy. Yet the intellectuality of scholars does not go wasted. They now help the acquisitors stay in power by doing what they do best—devising dogmas that, in return for some compensation, justify the rule of acquisitors. This they accomplish, as always, in a way that lures the gullible—by concealing their support for the acquisitor's primacy in the garb of individual rights, liberty, and justice. In reality, however, such lofty principles are openly violated: They are usually observed when it serves the interests of the affluent. Once the scholars give in, warriors and laborers also perform services for the rich. Thus in the acquisitive age, all other sections submit to the wealthy who then control the means of production—land, factories, financial capital. Feudalism and capitalism, for instance, are two pointed examples of the acquisitive era of western civilization.

Of all forms of government, the one loved by the opulent is that where the central authority is the weakest. In the military era this is impossible. In the intellectual's era the central power is not so strong, but the rigid social codes that the scholars contrive to control people keep a tight leash on acquisitive minds. That is why one finds that the acquisitive era, especially as it matured, was accompanied by a high degree of decentralized political authority in every civilization. A centralized system can, if it suits its purpose, force the rich to share their wealth with the poor, and no one is more aware of this risk than the acquisitors. Therefore, whenever the wealthy hold the reins, the system of government as well as the administrative apparatus are decentralized over time.

One distressing feature of the epoch of the affluent is that the virus of acquisitive mentality eventually infects all sections of society. Attitudes of the ruling class do not spread so much, do not become so pervasive in other eras; but in the age dominated by the wealthy, the distinct marks of other groups ultimately submit to the glitter of money. Everything is commercialized as a result—music, art, literature, sports.

Crime also begins to flourish. A general disregard for the rule of law developed in all acquisitive periods; all sorts of crimes—murders, thefts, muggings, rape—then plagued the public in every civilization. Family ties too became loose. At some places, this was reflected in repugnant harems of the noblemen, at others in increased frequency and social tolerance of divorce.

Prostitution, which was born in the intellectual's era, undergoes a remarkable growth in the acquisitive age. Those who have money to burn are able to corrupt many poverty-stricken women. And once the ruling class casts off moral scruples, other sections are quick to follow suit. As a consequence, moral degeneration comes to pervade the entire society. This results not only from the lewdness of men, but also from the looseness of family ties, excessive stress on individualism, and a general lack of social discipline that springs inevitably from a decentralized political structure.

As time passes, increasing amounts of wealth end up in the hands of the rich, and the acquisitive era gradually drifts toward the lawlessness of the laborer age. Eventually, things become so wretched that some angry warriors and intellectuals rise in rebellion and with the help of laborers bring an end to the age of acquisitors. Soon afterwards, the rebellious warriors take over and the civilization moves afresh on the track of social cycle.

Process of Social Change

Sarkar's law of social change states that power and influence shift from one group to another in accordance with a certain pattern. Several questions come to mind at this point. First, is the change from one era to another smooth and peaceful, or is it violent and marked by bloodshed? Second, how do stages of rise and fall of a group behave within each era? Is this rise or fall continuous or subject to cycles as well?

It should be noted at the outset that every entity, however small or large, is subject to cycles. Everything in this universe, no matter how short or long its life, moves with ups and downs. Nothing moves in a straight line. Everybody can see this in his own life. One day a person is happy, another day unhappy. Things are going well today, they may go sour tomorrow. Everything in this world is therefore subject to fluctuations.

The shift in power and prestige from one group to another itself represents cyclical movement of society. But within each era also the dominating class is subject to oscillations. The group in command may be temporarily dethroned, but if its attitudes continue to prevail among people, then it will soon come back to power. For example, suppose society is passing through the acquisitive age. Suddenly there is a military coup and the army takes over the government. If acquisitive mentality continues to dominate people, soon the wealthy will return to prominence. Thus, within each era also, the reigning group's fortunes are subject to cycles. But in any age, named according to the dominant mentality, the ruling group stays in power much longer than any other class. A close analysis of civilizations reveals that during any era the dominant class remains on top for at least two-thirds of that period. For instance, if an intellectuals' era lasted for 300 years, one would find that the scholars during that period ruled for at least 200 years and other groups for at most 100 years.

All this suggests that at times one may not be able to recognize the particular epoch of any society. The fact that nothing moves in a straight line does present difficulties. But a serious student should be able to see where a society stands at any moment of time. The following points should be borne in mind in the study of history:

1. In any society spread over several regions, one should first identify the most important region. For instance, in Western civilization, which is spread among many nations, America today is the most influential country. Since the U.S. is now passing through the laborer age which is marked by high crime, extreme materialism, generally loose morals, excessive individualism, we will say that the entire Western world is in the laborer age. It is possible that some regions of a society may differ from the most important nation. But that does not count. What counts is the dominant mentality in the dominant region of a society. For instance, Canada, another member of Western civilization, is still in the acquisitive age. It does not suffer from high crime. However, today, the character of Western society as a whole is determined not by the ruling mentality in Canada, but by that in the U.S.

2. There may be more than one important region in a civilization at any moment of time. Then the

class ruling in the majority of such regions determines the character of that society.

3.	Once dominant regions in a society have been identified, the next step is to see which group is in power in those regions. Normally one should be able to pinpoint the class controlling the government either directly or indirectly. That is to say, one should be able to see if warriors, intellectuals or acquisitors enjoy the political power. For instance, a centralized government with absolute authority usually means that either warriors or intellectuals are at the helm.

However, if it is not clear which group dominates politics, one should examine the ideology popular in society. What do the theories say? Do they favor a militaristic attitude of adventure and fearlessness, or a scholar's interest in otherworldliness and in theories for the sake of theories, or an acquisitor's materialism over the intellectual or adventurous pursuits of mind?

4.	Another way to identify an era in society is to observe what an average person wants to become, what career he wants to choose. Does he seek a career in the army, or does he want to become a scholarly theologian, priest or a statesman, or does he aspire to be a big landlord, banker, merchant, or businessman? In any society the profession of the ruling class is the one most sought by the public. In the military age, an average man generally dreams of becoming an army officer. In the intellectual's age, he likes to become an influential scholar, a high-priest or an adviser to the apparent but nominal ruler. In the acquisitive age, by contrast, an average person seeks to become a merchant, businessman, feudal landlord or financier. In the laborer age, people usually become lazy, extremely materialistic and greedy. They then like to become wealthy without working hard.

Each era moves through five stages—infancy, youth, maturity, senility and death. During infancy and senility, the ruling group faces many challenges and may be temporarily thrown out of power. But during youth and maturity, there is a good deal of social and political stability. The government is then relatively benevolent, and society evolves at a fast pace. However, successive generations of the dominant class, having been nurtured in luxury, turn oppressive and tyrannical. They care nothing for the rights and feelings of their people. That is when new conflicts develop in society and the fortunes of the rulers begin a long-term decline. Old age sets in, and the era meets its end usually in violence but at times in a peaceful manner.

Those opposing the establishment then come to power and start another age, with a new ideology and new attitudes.

This is the process that manifests itself time and again in the course of social evolution from the warrior era to the intellectual's era and then to the acquisitive age. Whereas in all phases of civilization, society consists of four broad sections, at the end of the acquisitive era only two remain: acquisitors and laborers—warriors and intellectuals having been reduced to the laboring class by the extreme concentration of wealth. For a long time in the acquisitive era, the standard of living remains high and the public willingly provides services to the affluent to make a living. For a while, the entire social order works to support the dominance of the rich. The concentration of wealth, however, continues apace and since material resources available to society are limited, the acquisitors grow richer and richer only at the expense of other classes.

As wealth becomes concentrated, the living standard of the other three groups progressively declines, and there comes a time when society degenerates into two classes—the haves and the have-nots. So strong is the power of want and hunger that the distinctive features of the warrior's and intellectual's mind submit to the compulsions of survival. It is during such days that the laborer era is born. The resultant crime, poverty and malaise eventually invite the revolt of the masses who are led by the very warriors and scholars—now diminished to the workman's ways of thinking—who had once received the acquisitive system with open arms. Sarkar calls this revolution the laborer revolution, one that occurs in the terminal phase of the acquisitive era, contributes towards its end and is brought about by disgruntled warriors and intellectuals.

The laborer revolution reflects not the fact that it is engineered by the laboring class, which is generally unable to lead, but the fact that it is masterminded by those reduced to the laborer's level of poverty. Few warriors and scholars then remain, for, forced to devote all their time to make a living, they have little time for activities of adventure and art. It is at such times that the laborer revolution occurs, and the influence of wealth is swept aside. In the ensuing polity, which may arise immediately or after a brief interlude of adjustment, power reverts to the warriors.

Western Society

Let us now explore the annals of Western society and see if it has indeed evolved in terms of the law of social cycle.

Students of Western Civilization generally begin its study with the Greco-Roman era, although some trace it back to the Minoan period and then to the Neolithic age in Europe and the island of Crete. Proponents of the latter view are, however, in minority, for earlier civilizations were strikingly different, and in any case there is not that much known about the ancient European world. Let us then begin with the year one.

To understand the evolution of the West, it is necessary to have some background of the social structure of the Roman Empire, because even though that society has long been dead, Roman Law, the Latin literature and some other Latin institutions have survived till this day. At the dawn of first century A.D., the warrior era can be seen to be prevailing in the Empire with Augustus as its Imperator or Emperor enjoying supreme command over the military and provinces. This is the age of absolutism and the tradition of conquests continues unabated. The chief bequest of the so-called Principate, said to have begun with the ascendance of Augustus, is the Roman Law which, among other things, affirmed that all humans are by nature equal and have certain fundamental rights that no governments are entitled to transgress.

The system of absolutism reached its zenith in 284 A.D. with the accession of Diocletian. Prior to his reign, the ruler, at least in theory though not in fact, was an agent of the people who had some fundamental rights, but now even that semblance of "responsible" government disappeared. The main reason for this change lies in the economic decline of the third century; the people having lost confidence in themselves were ready to forfeit all their rights for the elusive hope of peace and security.

Despotism, however, could only temporarily arrest the downfall of the Roman Empire whose economic and social structure had already been enfeebled by the decline in agriculture, population, commerce, and cities. The lack of a law of succession periodically gave rise to bloody conflicts at the time of the ruler's death, and the resulting degeneration of the army only accentuated the decay. It was at this time that the Christian religion gained a foothold in society. The Catholic Church succeeded because it provided guidance and shelter to the oppressed at a time when the Roman Empire was crumbling under the weight of imperialism as well as invading hordes who pounced on the spoils from all directions—Northern Europe, the Eurasian Steppe, the Arabian Peninsula, the Atlas and the Sahara.

In accordance with Sarkar's law of social cycle, the Church in any case would have inherited power from the Roman Empire, but the latter's downfall was hastened by the onslaught of Barbarian invasions, which led to a lot of bloodshed, pillage and violence. Had it not been for Christianity, Western Civilization would have met its grave at that time; under the spate of invading marauders, the decadent Roman society could have died, were it not for a little life-breath that vibrated the budding Church. This is how the era of intellectuals, represented by the Pope and bishops, was born.

At first, of course, Christianity had to struggle against tremendous odds. It is true that older forms of paganism in Rome were losing ground during the first three centuries, but this did not necessarily spell triumph for the religion of Christ. The Imperial Government either supported or tolerated many other cults and beliefs from the East. However, with the decline in the social fiber, Christianity, in spite of tough competition from other religions, spread quickly, and by the time of Diocletian's coronation, Christian communities were organized in nearly every city of the Empire. Even the periodical official persecution of Christians could only slow, but not stop, the eventual triumph of Christianity over all other faiths. Most of its early converts were gained from the slaves and laboring classes.

In the first three centuries, Christianity genuinely embodied the teachings of Christ whose magnetic and selfless life-story dominated the preachings. This was the main source of strength in the admirable lives led by the early saints. With the passage of time, however, especially after Christianity was recognized as the official religion of the Empire towards the end of the fourth century, the Church too succumbed to luxury and bigotry. Having gained official recognition, the Church no longer remained the religious society of the poor and the middle class. In order to acquire wealth and general acceptance, it subordinated principles to politics and secular affairs. Its bishops and saints were now interested more in perpetuating their positions and privileges than in living up to sublime and lofty ideals. Instead of society depending on the Church for moral guidance, the Church became a parasite on society.

During the latter part of the fourth century, the Church gained ground because the king had been converted to Christianity. This was a marked reversal from the older days of persecution, because now the ruler himself encouraged enrichment by the priesthood. By the fifth century, the clergy had become the dominant social and even political power of the Empire. In the name of the warrior king, it was the Church—headed by a Pope, bishops and priests—that then ruled society. The age of intellectuals thus began in the fifth century.

At the behest of the clergy, the government acted to root out paganism, its rituals and sacrifices, although later the Church itself felt it necessary to devise rituals and dogmas of its own.

The intellectual's age in the West lasted from the middle of the fifth century to about the end of the ninth. During these four hundred years, priests completely controlled society, with only periodic opposition from the warriors. One such warrior was Emperor Charlemagne who reigned from 768 to 814. During his rule, Charlemagne not only conquered many territories, but he also took over the Church, thereby temporarily establishing the era of warriors. Other than that, the clergy had few rivals for over four centuries. The priest ruled with the help of his dogmas which portrayed him an intermediary between common man and God. This is precisely how intellectuals govern. Their theories enable them to trap society in the web of complex but self-serving rules and regulations.

It is during the intellectual's age that women lost their high social status that they had enjoyed during the Roman Empire. During the preceding age of warriors, women had led a very active life. They participated in social, economic and political events. But as soon as the priesthood took over, woman came to be regarded as inherently evil and a temptress. Man's purpose was then to serve God, but woman's to inflate the heart of man. While priests were not sure if woman had a soul, they proclaimed man to be God-Almighty to his wife. One effect of all these attitudes was that rape or prostitution became solely the fault of woman [1, Ch. 5]. And in this respect what happened in Western society, was repeated verbatim in all civilizations.

The intellectual's age lasted until the end of the ninth century, when a series of events led to the ascendancy of feudal landlords, culminating in Feudalism. The rule of intellect and theories then gave way to the rule of wealth. Intellectuals then became subservient to the landlords who possessed the acquisitive mentality. Scholars now justified the supremacy of landed magnates in terms of a new theory called the Christian paternalistic ethic.

The era of acquisitors lasted from the start of the tenth century to about the middle of the fourteenth, when some unforeseen events, such as the Bubonic Plague of 1348, the Hundred-Years War between England and France, brought about the laborer age or the era of conflict between ruling acquisitors and the serfs. This was a period of unprecedented crime and near anarchy in Europe. Peasants and lords fought pitched battles, resulting in bloodshed and violence.

The laborer age, which is usually short-lived, lasted for a hundred years, till about the middle of the fifteenth century when in a matter of 25 years social revolutions broke out in France, Spain and England. In the aftermath of these revolutions, warriors came back to power, bringing about another period of absolutism.

The second military age of the West began around 1460 when Louis XI defeated nobles in France and established a centralized monarchy. In Spain this task was accomplished by Queen Isabela and Prince Ferdinand in the 1470s, whereas in England absolutism reemerged in 1485 with the rise of Henry VII who founded the Tudor dynasty. This is how the second social cycle began in the West.

The new warrior age lasted till 1689 when an historic event in England, called the Glorious Revolution, overthrew the reigning monarch. The intellectuals then came to power again, but this time in the guise of the prime minister who, of course, ruled only indirectly—in the name of the new king. During the early seventeenth century, the primacy of intellectuals reappeared in other important areas of Europe as well. In France, following the death of Louis XIV, the kings were extremely feeble, and their imperium was actually enjoyed by their council of ministers. In Central Europe, then ruled by the Austrian House of Hapsburg, the role of the prime minister was filled by the State Chancellors who overshadowed their kings and queens.

The second age of intellectuals lasted till the 1860s, when the New Industrial Revolution brought capitalists to the forefront of society. Businessmen, bankers and merchants, who possess acquisitive mentality, then came to prominence. Acquisitors have been ruling the West ever since.

Today, Western society is passing through another laborer age. That is why there is so much conflict between wealthy corporations and labor unions, something reminiscent of the conflict between landlords and peasants during Feudalism; that is why there is so much crime, drug and alcoholic addiction, materialism and general malaise in society today.

This state of affairs cannot last long. Social conflict in the West will continue to grow until the influence of affluence is eliminated. Society will then move into another age of warriors. (See [1, Ch. 9] for further details on this point).

3

The Long-Run Cycle of Money Growth in the United States

Towards the end of the previous Chapter I argue that ever since the second half of the 19th century, Western society has been moving through the age of acquisitors, where men of affluence hold the reins. Dominion of the ruling class then stems from its control over wealth as well as the means of production, while all other classes—the warriors, the intellectuals, the laborers—readily submit to the affluent elite. It is in this era that the system of government is extremely decentralized and, as a consequence, crime flourishes, families break down, and extreme greed and individualism come to permeate the social order. Such a socio-economic system prevailed in the West in the second half of the Middle Ages and is generally called feudalism; today it prevails again and is called capitalism.

This chapter provides some empirical evidence for Sarkar's law of social cycle. Specifically, it presents data demonstrating that at least U.S. society has evolved through the acquisitive age ever since Independence. In the process, a few myths popular among economists also come to light.

Western Society and the United States

Before turning to the empirical evidence, it is necessary to see how capitalism has evolved, especially in the United States of America, which is among the youngest offshoots of Western Civilization. The United States is currently the nerve-centre of capitalism, and its history deserves a separate treatment.

In terms of Sarkar's thesis U.S. history presents few complications. It is easy to see that right from the influx of Europeans to the North American continent, U.S. has been moving through the acquisitive age. This is not to suggest that capitalism has always prevailed in the U.S. society, only that right from its inception the forces of wealth have been predominant. Prior to the American Civil War (1861-5), landed proprietors of great wealth were in command of society and government, but since then social supremacy has belonged to owners of financial capital and industries. Thus, in one form or another, the affluent have dominated U.S. society right from its birth, and this signifies the long continuance of the acquisitive age.

Although it is customary to commence U.S. history from 1492, the fateful year in which Columbus discovered America, American settlements really began with 1607 when an English merchant company arrived at Jamestown and founded the colony of Virginia. Another colony was established in 1620 at Plymouth—this time by the Pilgrims who left England to avoid the persecution of James I and the Anglican Church. These two experiments were merely the beginning of what turned out to be a steady stream of immigrants sailing from Europe, especially England, to America. Within a century, thirteen-odd English colonies were established along the Atlantic coast of North America. In addition, Spain and France occupied remnants of what today is U.S. mainland.

Europeans came to settle in the colonies for a wide variety of reasons. Some groups such as the Pilgrims, Puritans, Quakers, Jews, Roman Catholics and Huguenots came for the sake of freedom in their religious practices. Others like the English merchants were lured by trade and good economic prospects. Most of the early settlers were determined to assert religious and economic freedom. Having suffered much at home, they were not inclined to accept monarchy or any other autocratic government in the colonies. They had come as private groups of people, and, except in the earliest years, they did not regard themselves as agents of the British king or of anyone else who could command them from home. For all these reasons, the system of government that developed in the colonies was from the earliest far more representative than its British counterpart. Even as England chafed under the autocracy of Stuart kings, the colonists enjoyed some form of democratic government.

The basic structure of colonial governments resembled the British archetype. Each colony was headed by a governor, appointed either by the king or, as in Maryland, Delaware and Pennsylvania, by private proprietors who, in hopes of high profits, had decided to attempt settlement in the New World. The governor was advised by an appointed council and a lower house, which was elected by those who satisfied certain property qualifications. In theory, therefore, each colonial government could have been an autocracy dominated by the governor or the proprietor, but in practice the real power gradually passed to elected legislators, who were either owners of vast estates, or, as in New England, wealthy merchants. And several reasons were responsible for this shift of power.

Most proprietors who obtained charters from the king had grandiose visions of royal prerogatives and authority. They had hoped to impose on their colonies the same social stratification as characterized England, where land was scarce and a landed magnate a man of influence in society. Conditions, however, were very different in America, which was one vast expanse of unmolested land. Any repressive system based on the relationship between landlords and landless peasants was simply doomed to failure in the New World, because if a person disliked living under one proprietor, he could move elsewhere. It is not then surprising that as economic enterprises most proprietorships proved to be colossal failures. Hence, in most colonies, one by one the proprietors relinquished their claims to the royal authority.

While the proprietors were unsuccessful in establishing political oligarchy, the governors did not have much luck either. In principle they had veto power over all legislation enacted by their legislative assemblies, but in practice they could do little but treat the legislators with deference. This is because the assemblymen came to control the allocation of revenues; even the governor's salary depended upon their appropriations. Thus the power of the purse generally prevailed over the threat of veto, and the colonists deftly employed it to run their affairs: They were masters in their own land.

Another experiment at some kind of centralized government was made in Massachusetts, which was founded in 1629. This was an attempt to establish a theocracy—a government based on religious tenets. Massachusetts had been early settled by a group of English Puritans, men and women imbued with evangelical zeal, who, having been deprived of their visions in the mother country, now hoped to build a Christian commonwealth on the new soil. It is not that the Puritans displayed tolerance for other faiths, only that they sought to found a society of like-minded, God-fearing people. In their system, the civil authority was supposed to submit to dictates of the Church. The Puritan regime did prevail for a while, but it was doomed to failure for the same reasons that subverted the proprietors' attempts to found an oligarchy. As the colonists moved from coastal areas to the interior, some of the early religious zeal waned, and economic concerns in the harsh, unfamiliar environment began to take precedence. As the economy grew over time, religious matters were subordinated to mundane affairs. Even though religion and the clergy continued to have some sway, by the eighteenth century the theocratic experiment in Massachusetts died under the unrelenting onslaught of improving economic conditions.

A similar fate awaited the later theocratic experiments in Rhode Island and Pennsylvania. There, too, economic concerns eventually prevailed over the sagging currents of religion, resulting in some kind of democratic government. The crux of my argument so far is that all attempts to found a centralized regime eventually failed in colonial America. By the eighteenth century, representative governments were established in all English colonies with varying, but mostly nominal, degrees of intervention by the Church in secular affairs.

Colonial American society is quite often pictured as a homogeneous community with few of the class conflicts that bedeviled contemporary Europe. This was perhaps true of the early settlements, but as the abundance of natural resources led to high economic growth, social stratification resulted from differing individual fortunes. The early settlers tended to have an advantage over the latecomers, as the former occupied the best and well-located tracts of land. In any case even though few aristocratic families migrated from England to American colonies, and even though most colonists brought with them little wealth, a native aristocracy, based on wealth differentials, did develop by the eighteenth century. In America, unlike contemporary England, capital and labor were extremely scarce, but land and natural resources abundant. In England wealth belonged to capitalists, in America to owners of vast estates, especially those in the Middle and Southern colonies. It was mainly in New England, which throve on trade and commerce, that wealthy merchants appeared, and there, unlike contemporary Europe, no stigma was attached to income derived from interest and profit.

Regardless of the source of wealth, those who owned it commanded great esteem and influence even in colonial America. The office that an average American then coveted was the governor's council, which was composed mainly of the richest men in the land. Appointed for life, the councilmen participated in the making of laws as well as in executive decisions. In the fullness of time, the governors and their councils were overshadowed by the elected legislative assemblies, but the assemblymen too were far from men of humble means. This sway of opulence in early American life emerges strikingly in the words of Charles A. and Mary R. Beard:

> In each colony the representative assembly, by whatever process instituted, was elected by the property owners. The qualifications imposed on voters were often modified but in every change the power of property . . . was expressly recognized. In the South, where agriculture was the great economic interest, land was the basis of suffrage; Virginia, for example, required the elector in town or country to be a freeholder, an owner of land—a farm or a town lot of a stated size. Where agriculture and trade divided the honors, politics reflected the fact; in Massachusetts, for instance, the suffrage was conferred upon all men who owned real estate yielding forty shillings a year income, or possessed other property to the value of £40. [5, pp. 109-110].

Thus, right from the beginning the American society has evolved in terms of the acquisitive age, and although religion also played a strong role in early settlements, its influence was soon swept aside by the rising tide of economic growth and prosperity. Does this in any way contradict my conclusion reached in Chapter 2 that the eighteenth century of Western Civilization belongs to the intellectual's age? In other words, does the acquisitive era of the eighteenth-century American society, an offspring of Western Europe, nullify the result already obtained? It does not.

The earlier result is at most weakened somewhat but not negated, for several reasons. One reason concerns the population. U.S. population, though growing at astronomical rates, was for a long time just a fraction of the population of England and France. It is only after 1850 that America overtook either in this regard. Another reason concerns U.S. influence in Western society in which England and France were dominant until the end of the nineteenth century. It is not until the turn of the twentieth century that the U.S. assumed leadership of the Western world. The industrial revolution had originated in England, but by the late nineteenth century America had far surpassed every European nation in industrial might. Capitalism had its roots in the British soil, but it is in America that it attained its biggest triumphs, its full bloom. In the arena of international politics also, U.S. actions, especially its victories in Hawaii, Cuba and the Philippines, then caught the attention of European imperialist powers. Thus it is only towards the end of the nineteenth century that America began to affix its stamp on the West, and by then the leading nations of Western Europe, such as England and France, had moved into the acquisitive age. Thus the fact that America, even in its formative phase, had begun with the acquisitive era, while its European parents were moving through the warrior or intellectual's age, does not in any way impair the validity of the law of social cycle for Western Civilization. The U.S. then was not what it is today.

Going back to U.S. history, the thirteen American colonies, strewn across the Atlantic coast, remained under the formal dominion of Britain until 1776, when a series of British policies designed to squeeze more taxes out of the colonies led to their revolt. Out of that revolutionary turmoil, an American nation was born. It is then that the democratic forces got a new shot in the arm, but the hegemony of wealth continued. The independent country made a fresh start by adopting a new constitution, which on the whole has served it well to this day. Three different branches of government—legislative, executive, and judicial—were established, with each serving as a check on the potential abuse of power by the other two. Within a few years, a Bill of Rights guaranteeing some fundamental rights to all people, not just the citizens, was added to the original Constitution. In this bill, the acquisitor's imprint can be clearly seen. While it contained some human rights such as the freedom of worship, speech, the press, and petition among others, it ignored the fundamental human right to work and employment. Yet the unlimited right to private property was duly included.

Even though U.S. Constitution did not then establish a democracy based on universal suffrage, as voting rights still derived from property qualifications, it was nevertheless the first experiment in history to ensure a rule of law and not of men and institutions. In practice, of course, the intent of this noble document was frequently flouted, for its enforcement was still left to men, yet it was more humanitarian than any other set of principles guiding contemporary governments. True it was unable to abolish slavery of the black people, but slavery had been a relic of pre-Independence times. Ultimately, however, the Constitution did play a role in its abolition. True, it was not without a frightful civil war (1861-5) that Abraham Lincoln, a man of great courage and boundless love for people, could finally exorcise the nation from the curse of slavery; yet it is under the auspices of the Constitution that Lincoln, born of ordinary parentage, could in the first place become U.S. President. Thus U.S. Constitution is a magnificent document that can take credit for many admirable achievements, but it has also been often abused by large corporations.

One notable instance of this abuse immediately comes to mind. Until the Civil War, land and natural resources were the main factors of production. While manufacturing was far from backward, agriculture had been the dominant sector until that time. This fact, of course, had been reflected in politics, as the political arena, with but few exceptions, was a playground for landed magnates as late as the middle of the nineteenth century. Following the Civil War, however, the roles were gradually reversed. Although agriculture continued to grow, it failed to keep up with manufacturing, which became the major sector of the economy. This was not a sudden development, but a product of decades of rapid industrialization and capital accumulation. Politics too could not but reflect this gradual shift of economic power from landlords to businessmen and merchants. At the outset, there was only one political party—that of the Federalists—which was dominated by landed interests with no effective opposition. The birth of the modern system of two parties, each with distinctive programs, styles and policies, is a later development which reached its culmination in 1854, when the Democratic party, formed earlier in 1825, was opposed by the Republican party. However, while both political parties differed from each other in significant ways, they both gradually came into the hands of business magnates, financiers and merchants. And it is they who used the Constitution to their own advantage.

Following the Civil War, Congress (U.S. legislative assembly) passed the first Civil Rights Act as the Fourteenth Amendment to the Constitution. Ostensibly, American Blacks were to be major beneficiaries of this law, which granted them citizenship and equal rights and forbade any state government from taking away the life, liberty, or property of any person without due process of law. However, for several decades the Fourteenth

Amendment did little to protect the civil rights of American Blacks, who were forced to live in misery, squalor and poverty—hardly better than slavery. Instead, the Amendment became a handy tool in the hands of big business for self enrichment. Most state courts ruled that corporations were persons and therefore entitled to protection under the due process clause. Each time a state government passed legislation to curb the anti-social practices of a corporation, federal courts would step in and proclaim state regulations unconstitutional, contending that the latter flouted the "due process" clause of the Amendment. State governments thus became helpless before the might of giant enterprises.

Unencumbered by any state intervention, and with the federal government at their beck and call, corporations throve in America as never before. The economy grew at an unprecedented rate, while small businesses were gobbled up by a few giants. The wheeling and dealing that went on among businessmen towards the end of the nineteenth century have earned them the label of Robber Barons, men who, according to Fite and Reese, "built poor railroads, turned out shoddy products, cheated honest investors, sweated labor, and exploited the country's natural resources for their own wealth and satisfaction". [13, p. 355]. Almost every major industry became a monopoly. The economy might not have grown as fast without them, but there were certainly distressing side-effects of this concentration of economic power on so vast a scale—a malady that U.S. society has never since been able to shake off. So outrageous were their practices that by 1889 the whole country was up in arms. In response, Congress passed the Sherman Antitrust Act, which barred any person or corporation from conspiring to form monopolies or to stifle competition in any way. This, however, turned out to be a carrot dangled by the business-dominated Congress before an aroused public. As with the Fourteenth Amendment, this Act too was eventually used by corporations to their own advantage.

For the next few decades, the Sherman Act was interpreted by the courts in a way that emasculated labor unions. Their strikes were ruled as anti-competitive practices. Thus a law meant to soothe the public ire eventually became an anti-labor law.

What producers detest most is competition among themselves, for competition increases uncertainty and trims profits. They are also, in general, wary of governmental intervention and regulations, lest their earnings are adversely affected. Regulation, of course, is welcome to them if it cuts competition and ensures a steady and high return. Towards the end of the nineteenth century, while most industries became concentrated in the hands of a few barons, railroads continued to be competitive. In fact, the competition there was so intense that they themselves demanded regulation from Congress, which, of course, was quick to oblige them. In response to their appeals, Congress in 1887 established the Interstate Commerce Commission (ICC) to regulate the railroads in the public interest. Thus one might say that from the Civil War down to the fateful year of 1929, the year of the greatest economic depression, the acquisitive era in the U.S. was at its zenith. Big business flourished on all fronts: On the one hand, feeble anti-trust laws like the Sherman Act provided the smokescreen under which monopolies, oligopolies and trusts could flourish while labor unions remained on the leash; on the other, various regulatory commissions such as the ICC were instituted to eliminate competition among oligopolies, which seemed unable to collude and thus act in unison as a monopoly. One by one, competition, the bane of exuberant profits, was smothered in virtually all industries. Since then the covert collusion between the government and big business has steadily increased as the latter can earn monopoly profits with the blessing of various regulatory agencies, which are often composed of hirelings of the very industries they are supposed to regulate.

That capitalism is subject to unique internal traumas had been fathomed by Marx long before other economists began to diagnose this malady, whose symptoms were discernible as early as the birth of the republic. U.S. capitalism was in its infancy when it had its first bout with economic depression in 1782; it weathered that storm, only to be hit by it again and again. In all, during the first half of the nineteenth century, it encountered four economic crises; during the second half, however, it encountered five (in 1854, 1857, 1873, 1884, and 1893). The twentieth century opened with brighter prospects, but the jinx of depression would not release the economy. After giving a mild foretaste of its impending assault in 1907, 1921 and 1927, the jinx struck with a vengeance on October 24, 1929—the day of the Great Crash. On that day, the bottom fell out of stock prices on the New York Stock Exchange. The downward spiral of security prices that then began quickly engulfed the American economy, and eventually the entire capitalist world. Economic catastrophe of the Great Depression cannot be easily pictured. Within three years, there were 85,000 business failures in America, and twelve million people, equal to 25 percent of the labor force, became unemployed. The brunt of the lay-offs, of course, fell on the Blacks who had been exploited ever since colonial times.

The economic blight spread overnight to other troubled nations linked with American economy through international commerce. The entire Western world then stood on the verge of collapse. The apocalyptic Marxian vision of the demise of capitalism seemed closer to fruition than ever before. But then came a brilliant economist, John Maynard Keynes, and the Second World War. Keynes prescribed the medicine, while the war served to show that it could work. Under the enormous government expenditures occasioned by the war, unemployment slowly disappeared, and, for a while, gave way to shortages of labor. Keynes had recommended massive doses of government spending to combat unemployment, and the war proved him right. Ever since, Keynesian economic theory and its offshoots have been largely guiding the Western world.

Under the watchful eyes of Keynesian policies, capitalism seemed to be operating smoothly for a full quarter of a century following the Second World War. There were mild relapses occasionally, but no duplication of the 1929 tragedy. But just when the war against economic crises seemed to have been won, another intractable problem, potentially more dangerous than large-scale unemployment, cropped up and has persisted since 1969—namely the coexistence of inflation with a high level of unemployment. This problem eluded Keynes, for there is supposed to be a trade-off between unemployment and inflation in the Keynesian system: both cannot rise or decline at the same time. As yet there is no consensus among economists—and there hardly ever is—as to how the new challenge should be met. Not that the problem has faded away, just that it admits of no simple, and politically feasible, solution.

On top of all these troubles, in 1973 the world economy was jolted by an international cartel called the Organization of Petroleum Exporting Countries (OPEC). There was a four-fold rise in oil prices as a result, and U.S. economy tottered once again. The recession of 1973-5 was the steepest since the Great Crash, but more than that it was accompanied by an unprecedented double-digit inflation. Keynesian remedies were applied again, and as a consequence the economy recovered, only to be hit by a deadly stagflation lasting from 1980 to 82. Since then both inflation and unemployment have declined, but, as no fundamental reform has been undertaken, the crisis is still simmering, ready to erupt any moment.

Theories Underlying Capitalism

No socio-economic system can last long unless it rests on an appealing ideological structure. In this regard, capitalism is no exception. And, as with every elitist system, its ideological thread is sound in theory but tenuous in practice. Capitalism is defined as a social, economic and political system where the means of production- —industries, banks, natural resources, etc.—are owned by private corporations and individuals, where the political system operates primarily in the interests of such owners, and where the distribution of national income is determined by them. It is quite often associated with the free-enterprise system, which may be defined as one where businessmen, the owners of the means of production, are free to maximize their profits. This freedom in profit maximization is central to capitalism, for during the modern warrior and intellectual's eras, when state dominance and the Christian paternalistic ethic worked to condemn income from interest and profits, the prevailing economic systems were called mercantilism and "physiocratism". Industries and commerce existed even during those days, although not on so vast a scale; merchants did own financial capital, but the state did not permit them a free hand in making profit-maximizing decisions. Hence economists do not refer to those systems as capitalism: Aggrandisement of state income and power was then the chief concern of scholars. Thus the word "free" in the free-enterprise system refers really to the producer's freedom to maximize the return from his investment, and not, as many would have us believe, to the free operation of a market economy. The latter definition is only a special case of my definition, one that applies when perfect competition among businessmen prevails. The days of competition have long been gone, but capitalism continues to be called the free-enterprise system. This is because while competition is there no more, the producer's ability to increase his profits has soared more than ever before.

I have already noted that in an acquisitive era, scholars come forward to offer theories justifying the dominion of acquisitors. To the majority of intellectuals, it matters little how specious their justification is as long as it is catchy and acceptable to the system. Only a few advocate genuine reform and concern for the exploited, much to the dislike of the ruling class. It is in this broad perspective that the economic theory of capitalism propounded by Adam Smith, the father of economics, ought to be viewed. The period between 1500 and 1700 is traditionally associated with mercantilism, which apparently overlapped with the modern warrior age. It is during this period that the foundation for modern-day capitalism was laid. Yet the activities of merchants and industrialists were curbed by myriad state regulations. Even though many interest groups made a fortune from these regulations, the real driving force behind capitalism—the acquisitive instinct or the profit motive—was sanctioned neither by the state nor by the Church. Since the Church had submitted to the king, the responsibility for restraining the merchants from unbridled pursuit of self-interest fell on the crown. However, state regulations continued to derive from medieval ideology—the Christian paternalistic ethic.

Following the Glorious Revolution of 1689, dogmas exalting the power of state gave way to those exalting individualism and ultimately the acquisitive instinct. All this ferment occurred during the intellectual's era in which income from land commanded more moral and social prestige than income from usury and profit. Thus when Adam Smith wrote his masterpiece, *The Wealth of Nations,* in 1776, merchants and businesses, though not as encumbered by state regulations as during the preceding warrior era, were still not completely free to pursue their quest for profits. Smith's contemporaries sought refuge in the argument that human beings are moved primarily by selfish and egoistic motives; all human actions are rooted in self-preservation, and hence in egoism and self-interest.

Selfishness and avarice, therefore, are not vices but virtues for hard work and economic prosperity. By implication then, the state should keep its intervention in human activities to the minimum so that individual and social welfare is at the maximum.

This sanctification of greed and acquisitive behavior that had found support from the intellectuals—of whom many were employed by great trading enterprises—was readily embraced by the businesses. But its excessive stress on individualism produced apprehensions of anarchy in many minds. It is Smith's brilliant contribution that tended to calm their fears. His carefully thought-out analysis of the capitalist system, blessed with keen competition, removed from the doctrine of individualism many of its flaws that had worked to impede its general acceptance. Smith argues that, left to themselves, producers and workers are guided by self-interest to put their capital and labor to uses where they are the most productive. The mechanism which ensures this is the "invisible hand" of a free market where businessmen compete for consumers' money in an egocentric search for profits, and where consumers seek to obtain the best-quality product at the cheapest price. In quest of profit maximization, the producers are impelled to employ labor only in those goods for which there is demand, and to use productive techniques that are the most efficient so that unit costs are minimized. In a free-market economy, therefore, everyone is happy: while the producers earn maximum return, consumers are satisfied with a high-quality product available at the lowest price ensured by maximum productive efficiency. All this is the miracle performed by the "invisible hand" in spite of, or rather because of, relentless human greed and acquisitive behavior.

Smith thus assailed the myriad mercantilist regulations that had worked to perpetuate monopolies and further the interests of various groups. For monopolies destroy operation of the free market that ensures maximum social welfare. His work, therefore, was on the one hand a scathing denunciation of mercantilism, and on the other an eloquent plea for free enterprise or *laissez-faire*. However, the free-enterprise system that Smith had in mind condoned the producer's search for profit, but only in an environment characterized by keen competition among businessmen.

Not only do free markets generate maximum efficiency, they also, according to Smith, ensure a high rate of economic growth and hence a rising standard of living; because growth depends on capital accumulation, which in turn depends on the adequacy of profits. This is then another line of defense for acquisitive and self-serving behavior, for it ensures the continued economic progress of society. Thus growth and efficiency are the two pillars on which Smith based his eloquent plea of the free-enterprise system unencumbered by any state interference. Although his prognosis relied on the calculating instincts of individuals, it was also a moral indictment of mercantilism, which now stood exposed as a culprit impeding maximum social welfare. It is perhaps for this reason that his thought left its mark on writings for generations to come. Businessmen and laborers alike found passages in his work to support their own concerns.

The doctrine of *laissez-faire,* first propounded rigorously by Adam Smith and later refined by his disciples such as David Ricardo and J.B. Say, among others, is now known as the Classical theory of economics. With this economic ideology went a political creed that considered the state or government as a necessary evil—evil because of its encroachments on individual liberty, but necessary for an escape from anarchy. To government, Smith assigned three basic functions: justice, national defense, and the provision of certain public goods that are too unprofitable to be ever provided by private enterprise. This is a very general list of state functions, and although he denounced state patronage of economic interests in any form, his political ideas were seized by businessmen to justify government paternalism whenever they themselves were the beneficiaries.

At the time Smith wrote his book, capitalism was still in embryo. His vision of a competitive system where the consumer is sovereign, and where the powerless producer is scrambling to satisfy market demand and preferences did, to an extent, reflect economic reality. But by the late nineteenth century, capitalism had grown into adolescence. All over the West, especially in Germany and America, industrial colossi had sprung up to undermine the market mechanism that is supposed to maximize social welfare. While the forces of demand were free to operate, those of supply had been effectively constrained. But all this failed to deter a new breed of economists from erecting an even nobler defense of the free-enterprise system.

At precisely the time when the process of industrial concentration was under way, some economists, notably Jevons, Walras and Marshall among others, set out to clothe the classical economic ideology with an elaborate mathematical apparatus, while maintaining the assumption of perfect competition. Theirs is the so-called Neoclassical economic analysis, but in their basic theme of espousing *laissez-faire* they differ little from their precursors. Thus while the assumptions underlying capitalism had been drastically altered, economic theory emerged with a new make-up applied to the old face. Even as the Robber Barons were soaking away national wealth in their coffers, the Neoclassical economists recommended "hands-off" economic policies by the government, lest the giant corporations be inhibited from acting in the public interest.

The Neoclassical analysis presents the vision of an economy consisting of a large number of small producers and consumers, each unable to sway the market by himself. Unable to control market prices, businessmen can maximize profits only through maximum production at minimum costs. Motivated by self-interest, they hire factors of production from the households—land, capital, labor—in such a way that each factor is paid the value of what it contributes to the total product. Thus all factors, including producers, earn what they contribute to society—no less and no more. In such a frictionless world there is no possibility of any exploitation, for everyone earns what he deserves or what he contributes to society. There are no extortionate profits, for the very process of profit maximizing leads businessmen to earn no more than their social contribution. This is the Neoclassical vision of distributive justice.

On the side of demand, the Neoclassical economists suggest that each consumer seeks to maximize utility, which is quantifiable and depends upon the consumption of goods and services. In a free market economy the consumer, endowed with certain income and wealth and acting in self-interest, divides his spending among purchases of various commodities in such a way that his utility is maximized. Ultimately, utility maximization by each consumer means that, given the distribution of national wealth and income, social welfare, the sum total of all utilities, will be maximized. And not a step in this process needs help from the government. The Neoclassical economists thus raised the "invisible hand" of Adam Smith to an even nobler pedestal, added their own voice to the growing mystique of *laissez-faire*, while choosing to be deaf to deafening voices of surrounding reality. While the reality clamored for a diagnosis of the bulging concentration of economic power, of monopolies and trusts, of graft, wheeling-dealing and staggering corruption in the business arena, the economists confined themselves to their stylized, and idealized, conception of the world. The result was that their ideas, while far divorced from the earthly capitalist environment, were, and are, frequently used in the ideological defense of the supremacy of acquisitors.

While foundations of the Neoclassical economic theory were laid during the late nineteenth century, its progress and refinements continued well into the twentieth century and in fact they have continued, with brief interruptions, down to this day. In America a new generation of Neoclassical economists began to recognize some of the flaws in capitalism—namely the absence of perfect competition, under-production of socially desirable goods such as roads, parks, armies, etc., undesirable social externalities such as air pollution and a squalid environment, and above all, the economic depressions. But while such afflictions of capitalism were explicitly recognized, most economists reared in the Neoclassical tradition continued to regard them as aberrations tending to correct themselves. There were some who saw the need for serious governmental intervention to cure these socio-economic ills, but they were in a stark minority. As a result, the experts were ill-prepared to prescribe medicine for any economic cataclysm such as the one that beset the world in 1929. In short, the Neoclassical economists had undying faith in the ability of capitalism to pull itself out of any crisis as long as the state abstained from rendering help. For, in their view, official intervention could only make matters worse.

The Great Crash of 1929, therefore, caught economists napping in their idealized world. It was not supposed to last that long—not when the entire conventional wisdom was dead set against it. The entire Western world was then frightened not of any natural calamity, nor of any war on which the public wrath could be easily focused, but of the man-made calamity with no avenue of escape in sight. Before the medicine could be prescribed, the malady had to be properly diagnosed; venerated dogmas had to be discarded.

It was Keynes who set out to reshape and fundamentally reorganize economic theory to bring it in line with reality, which clamored for speedy treatment. In contrast to the major Neoclassical concern with microeconomics, i.e., with the economic behavior of individual economic units such as businessmen, consumers, etc., he addressed himself to the question of macroeconomics, i.e., with the analysis of the entire economy. Keynes observed that businesses perform two-pronged functions; as producers they supply goods; but simultaneously they pay incomes to factor-owners in the form of wages, rents, interest and profits. The factor-owners in turn spend money to buy goods from businessmen. There is thus a circular flow with money flowing from producers to consumers and then from consumers back to producers. As long as businessmen can sell all their goods at a reasonable profit, this circular process continues uninterrupted.

But several hitches may arise. A part of factor-incomes is saved and deposited with financial institutions, a part taken away by the government in the form of taxes, and a part spent on foreign goods in the form of imports. These are what we may call leakages from total expenditure, and they tend to keep aggregate demand for goods short of their aggregate supply. Counterbalancing these leakages are the three-pronged injections to total expenditure—business borrowing for investment, government spending, and exports. If the leakages are matched by injections, total spending matches the total value of goods produced, and the economy may be said to be in equilibrium, that is, it has no tendency to move up or down. If the leakages exceed injections, aggregate demand falls short of aggregate supply and some goods remain unsold, so that businessmen are forced to trim production and hence their employment of labor; in the opposite case of the injections exceeding leakages, national production and hence employment tend to rise.

This, in simple terms, is the well-known Keynesian process of national income determination. It is noteworthy that in this system spending or aggregate demand plays an active role, and aggregate supply a passive role in the sense that the latter converges to the former. High national income and hence high employment call for high aggregate demand. The implication is unmistakably clear: during years of low demand, the economy suffers from high unemployment and hence recessions or depressions. The policy prescription is also unmistakably clear: in order to cure unemployment, the government should step in and raise aggregate spending in the economy by means of fiscal and monetary policies.

Moreover, the state must constantly feel the economy's pulse. This is because business investment is a double-edged sword. On the one hand, investment expenditure contributes to total spending, thereby adding to aggregate demand, but on the other it adds to the economy's productive capacity and hence to its aggregate supply. Thus initially investment acts to balance demand with supply, but over the long run it tends to create an imbalance.

Furthermore, Keynes believed that those with higher incomes tend to save more than the poor, and this holds good for society as well. Thus with increased investment comes increased supply of goods and incomes, and eventually increased savings, which must be matched with ever increasing amounts of investment to avoid an excess supply of products. In other words, the growth process is explosive, as investment must rise each year to keep up with increasing levels of savings. But profitable investment outlets are in limited supply. So a time comes, when in order to eschew additional risks, businessmen curtail their investment. It is then that goods go unsold, and there begins a downward spiral, which halts only when national income has declined enough to generate a level of savings matching the reduced level of investment. Thus the government ought to keep an eye on the functioning of the economy, increasing aggregate demand in times of depression, and curtailing it in times of inflation. For to Keynes, the inflationary situation is just the opposite of the case of depression.

What kind of policies should the government follow? Here Keynes advocates a twofold attack in the form of fiscal and monetary policies. Fiscal policies involve the weighing of government expenditure versus tax receipts. During a depression, the fiscal policy calls for a budget deficit, i.e., for government expenditure to exceed the tax revenue; but with inflation the cure lies in a budget surplus. Monetary policy, by contrast, affects the economy indirectly—through its effect on business investment. Keynes argued that monetary expansion encourages investment, while a contraction discourages it. Hence during a depression, the monetary policy has to be expansionary, but during inflation, contractionary.

Keynesian economics is thus an antithesis of the Neoclassical ideology, for the government is now cast in the role of a constant watchdog indispensable to continued prosperity. The appeal of Keynesian theory lay in the fact that not only did it properly diagnose the economic ills, but it also advocated policies well within the reach of governments. For this reason its spread was swift and decisive, and, in spite of stubborn initial resistance from doctrinaire economists who detested any state intervention on purely ideological grounds, Keynes' thought soon displaced the ideas of his predecessors. Today it has become the orthodoxy to which challenges from other quarters are often posed. The most notable challenge was posed in the 1960s by the Nobel Laureate, Milton Friedman, who is credited with pioneering a whole new approach, called the monetarist approach, to the question of economic fluctuations under capitalism.

In a way, what Friedman has done most is to partially rehabilitate the neoclassical economic theory and philosophy. He may be regarded as the Adam Smith of the twentieth century, for he too has championed the philosophy of *laissez-faire* in the midst of an economic environment that has swerved away from it. Friedman argues that the source of most economic cycles is the monetary sector and not, as Keynes believed, the goods (or investment) sector; that is, the single most important determinant of the price level and employment is the level of money supply. While to Keynes the deficiency of investment relative to savings is the catalyst for recessions, to Friedman the causal factor is the change in the community's stock of money supply, whose growth, he argues, has shrunk prior to the advent of any recession in the United States [15]. Furthermore, this shrinkage in most cases resulted either from the inept actions of monetary authorities or from the intrusion of politicians. Unlike Keynes, therefore, he does not believe that it is possible to fine-tune the economy and still expect it to remain in good health. Government, to him, ought to be limited mainly to the protection of property rights, printing and managing money, courts, and the maintenance of law and order [14]. However, his writings touch not only on individual liberty but also on the rights of children and of lunatics.

The school of thought pioneered by Friedman is called Monetarism, which, as is now clear, differs fundamentally from Keynesian economics. Keynesians believe that the economy is basically unstable and the main source of instability is the level of investment. To stabilize the system, therefore, the government should actively intervene in the economy by following appropriate fiscal and monetary policies. This, in practice, has meant that the government should maintain high levels of budget deficit and money growth.

Monetarists, by contrast, argue that the economy is basically stable and government intervention does not help or, at worst, may itself be the cause of instability. The government, in their view, ought to restrain itself by balancing its budget over the business cycle and by permitting a monetary expansion at the annual rate of 4% or whatever is the long-run rate of growth of output. Implicit here is the belief that the authorities can control the supply of money, which to Monetarists, is the primary determinant of economic activity.

Sarkar and Monetarism

Let us now see what Sarkar's position is in this connection. From the viewpoint of the law of social cycle, expounded in Chapter 2, capitalism is synonymous with the West's second age of acquisitors and it is they who control the levers of not only the economy but of everything else in society.

To Sarkar, motion itself is systaltic or pulsative. Nothing moves in a straight line; every entity, animate or inanimate, evolves in a cyclical fashion. With a civilization, for instance, the law of social cycle, provides the rhythm.

Within each age, the ruling group also has its ups and downs, and its cycle determines the cycle of all other variables. The dominant class is the nucleus of society and around the cyclical fortunes of this nucleus revolve all social phenomena. During the acquisitive era, the power and prestige of the class atop the social hierarchy derives from its control and ownership of wealth. Under capitalism, for instance, the wealthy are supreme because they own a large portion of stocks, bonds, real estate and other means of production.

In the current age of acquisitors, the fortunes of businessmen, the dominant class, are associated with the supply of money. Under capitalism, money and wealth are closely related: They are almost synonymous. Since the wealthy are currently on top, and since money and wealth move together, under capitalism the supply of money must be the most important determinant of all social variables including the economy. This is simply an echo of Friedman's position, *but why money is the primary determinant of economic activity under capitalism can be explained only by Sarkar's hypothesis of social cycle.*

How can we prove this proposition? How can the doubts raised by Keynesian and other skeptics be resolved? In support of his view, Friedman cites the postwar behavior of the American economy, where annual fluctuations in the growth of both money and gross national product (GNP) have declined. Keynesians, however, have countered by arguing that first the money growth is hard to control, and second the change in GNP may be generating the change in money supply and not vice versa, so that money need not hold the pivotal position in the economy.

There is only one way to demonstrate peremptorily that money, nothing else, is the source of all oscillations under capitalism. And that is to pose the most difficult test. Since every entity is cyclical, the dominant entity also has a cycle. But this cycle must be rhythmical. This is because the primary variable must have an exact and stable cycle of its own. How else could it regulate the cycles of others? How else could it be dominant?

Thus, the test that we have posed is this. If money is the primary variable in society, its growth must follow a cyclical path of constant periodicity. Stated differently, unless the economy is completely traumatized, the cycle of money growth must hit either a peak or a trough every X number of years.

There can be no criterion tougher than this. Cycles of varying periodicity have been discovered for many variables in the past, but none displays the exactness demanded by the test posed above. If any such cycle exists, then it is a proof not only of the supreme position of that variable in society, but also of the broader concept of historical determinism underlying the law of social cycle. It may be noted at this point that our concern here is not with the time-path of money supply but with its growth. This is because we are analyzing an economy which has been growing over time.

The Cycle of Money Growth

Let us now examine the empirical evidence. From the data sources described in the appendix, one can obtain consistent estimates of money supply going as far back as the birth of the American nation in 1776. These figures, in the words of Friedman and Schwartz, "fragile as they may be, show no obvious discontinuity with the money-stock estimates for the century after 1867." [15, p. 259]. True, a little conjecture is involved in estimating money supply prior to 1800, but following that year many series are available, and that by Gurley and Shaw [17] comes very close to the methodology used by Friedman and Schwartz in obtaining statistics for later years. A simple transformation of these observations into rates of change per decade yields a vivid cycle presented in Chart 1. Here the decennial rate of money growth is defined as:

$$M^* = (M_t - M_{t-1}) \times 100/M_{t-1}$$

where M_t is money supply in decade t, specifically old M2, which is defined as currency in the hands of the public plus demand and time deposits with commercial banks, and M^* is the rate of growth of money. For example, the growth rate of money in the 1970s is given by:

$$M^*_{1970s} = \frac{\text{old M2 in 1980} - \text{old M2 in 1970}}{\text{old M2 in 1970}} \times 100$$

The money-growth cycle in Chart 1 begins with the 1770s, for no figures of any kind are available on money supply prior to that decade. But the 1770s, being the decade of American revolution, experienced extraordinary money growth. Even though precise earlier figures are unavailable, historians argue that money growth during the 1770s was the largest of all times in Colonial America.

Even a cursory examination of Chart 1 reveals that the decennial rate of growth of money has followed a long-run cycle, reaching a peak every third decade, with the singular exception of two decades following the Civil War of the 1860s.

Immediately after the Civil War, regarded as the most cataclysmic event in U.S. chronicle, the money-growth cycle is disrupted. Evidently the economy took about two decades to recuperate, but once the recovery was complete by the 1880s, the cycle resumed its rhythmical course, because within the next three decades money growth crested in the 1910s, which is the first peak decade of the 20th century. Thirty years later, the money-growth peak recurs in the 1940s and then again in the 1970s. If we were to plot the money-growth rate between 1980 and 84 and if such rates were to continue in the rest of the 1980s, we could obtain a point such as B, indicating that the 1970s were unmistakably the most recent peak of the cycle.

Thus Chart 1 shows that, except for the post-Civil-War interregnum, the decennial rate of growth of money crested every third decade over the past two centuries. This is an amazing feature of the U.S. economy never discovered before and it fits deftly with Sarkar's hypothesis that the dominant variable of any age follows a rhythmical cycle.

Why was the cycle disrupted in the aftermath of the Civil War? The reason is that the war left U.S. economy in a shambles. While every entity, according to Sarkar, follows a cyclical movement, its normal pattern is disturbed if it meets a major extraneous shock. It may then become comatose for a while; but after it recovers, it begins its normal cyclical pattern once again. What is important here is that the period of recuperation is followed by the same old rhythm, unless, of course, the entity dies.

This is precisely how U.S. economy behaved in the aftermath of the Civil War which, lasting from 1861 to 1865, shook the very foundations of American society, sending it into a coma for a while. While the South was devastated, the North suffered heavy damage from the loss of capital and skilled labor. Never before had the American nation been so traumatized, nor has it been ever since. Even the two world wars did not cause so much havoc and destruction, because they were fought on foreign soil.

It took the U.S. economy about two decades to recover, because from the 1880s onward the decennial rate of money growth resumed its cycle, reaching another peak in thirty

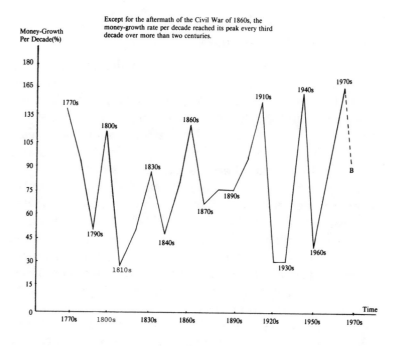

The Long-Run Cycle of Money Growth
Per Decade in the United States (1770s-1970s)

Except for the aftermath of the Civil War of 1860s, the
money-growth rate per decade reached its peak every third
decade over more than two centuries.

Money-Growth
Per Decade(%)

Chart 1

Source: 1) Friedman and Schwartz
        2) Ravi Batra

years in the 1910s. The three-decade cycle has continued ever since. In what follows, we ignore from our analysis the disruption of the money-growth cycle in the aftermath of the Civil War, assuming that such an event is not likely to recur in the near future.

Historical Determinism

What are the implications of the regularity of the long-run cycle of money growth displayed in Chart 1? First, as must be evident by now, money supply or wealth is the nucleus around which every other entity in society, not just the economy, revolves and has been so revolving at least since Independence. This implies that the United States has been in the age of acquisitors all this time.

Second, the cycle vividly illustrates the concept of historical determinism which has so often been ridiculed and reviled. That history follows a definite pattern can no longer be in dispute. There must exist an invisible hand weaving uneven historical threads into a smooth fabric. Economists of all stripes and persuasions agree that money supply is influenced by a large spectrum of forces seemingly unrelated to each other. How could they all get together and collude to follow a set path spanning more than two centuries? There must exist an invisible principle of Nature that brings order to the apparently disorderly currents in the annals of society. There must, for instance, exist a natural law that decides that the time has now come for money growth to soar, now to stabilize and now to fall.

The concept of historical determinism finds further support in the next two chapters which reveal that the long run decennial cycle of the type exhibited in Chart 1 also exists for at least two other variables, namely the rate of inflation and the degree of economic regulation by the government. Thus the money-growth cycle is no fluke, but has ample company.

Third, the Keynesians are correct in their claim that money supply cannot be controlled by authorities. Friedman argues for a fixed money- growth rule to be followed by the Federal Reserve System (or the Fed), which is the central bank in the United States. The Fed was established in 1914 mainly to bring the supply of money under control and to make the credit system respond speedily to changing business conditions.

Most economists attribute the decline of money growth in the 1980s to Paul Volcker, the Fed chief appointed in 1979, who restrained the engine of money supply in order to control inflation. However, the cycle of money growth reveals that Mr. Volcker was just an instrument in the hands of a natural law that guides the destiny of the American economy. There must be an invisible force, much like Adam Smith's invisible hand, that determines the time-path of money growth in the United States, and Mr. Volcker simply became a medium for the expression of its will. With the 1940s being the peak decade of money growth, the 1970s were destined to be the next peak decade of the three-decade cycle, so that the 1980s were pre-ordained to experience the fall in the growth of money. For the peak must obviously be followed by a decline.

What then is this invisible force? It is, according to Sarkar, the law of social cycle, which in turn is one facet of the generic principle of Evolution.

The Fed constitutes a milestone in the banking annals of the United States. Its purpose was to remedy a number of weaknesses that had plagued the economy since the establishment of the republic. Prior to the Fed, money supply responded only to conditions in the money market. One would think that the creation of the Fed would have at least tamed, if not eliminated, the money-growth cycle. Instead, it had just the opposite effect. Chart 1 reveals that the amplitude of fluctuations in the decennial rate of money growth was lower during the 19th century than during the 20th. Thus the creation of the Fed simply increased the long-run oscillations in money supply without in any way disrupting the pattern of the cycle.

Yet it is true that fluctuations in annual growth of money have declined since the 1940s. All this suggests that the Fed can leash money supply in the short run but not in the long run. In other words, man can control his destiny at a point of time but ultimately has to operate within certain bounds set by a supreme force—bounds which cannot be defied forever.

Finally, the money-growth cycle implies that capitalism is fundamentally unstable, and the creation of institutions such as the Fed, no matter how pioneering, cannot stabilize it. They are mere palliatives that in the long run actually destabilize the system. What is needed is not a perfunctory cure, but fundamental economic reforms, something that is discussed in Chapter 9.

Data Appendix

The data underlying Chart 1 can be obtained from Friedman and Schwartz [15], and Gurley and Shaw [17], or from Ravi Batra [2].

These data are presented in column 5 of Table I which is taken directly from Batra's article. The Table also contains figures for wholesale prices and inflation rates per decade, and these figures form the basis of analysis in the next chapter.

Table 1

Decennial average wholesale price index (1910-14) = 100, Old M2, Inflation Rates and Money Growth Rates

Decades	AP_t	M2(in billions of dollars)*	Inflation Rate in %	Money Growth in %
1740-1750	68	----	----	----
1750-1760	68	----	0	----
1760-1770	77	.004	13.2	----
1770-1780	116	.010	50.6	150.0
1780-1790	128	.0196	10.3	96.0
1790-1800	114	.030	-10.9	53.1
1800-1810	129	.067	13.2	123.3
1810-1820	144	.084	11.6	25.4
1820-1830	100	.126	-30.6	50.0
1830-1840	101	.232	1.0	84.1
1840-1850	84	.344	-16.8	48.3
1850-1860	97	.605	15.5	75.8
1860-1870	143	1.39	47.4	129.7
1870-1880	116	2.28	-18.9	64.0
1880-1890	91	3.99	-21.6	75.0
1890-1900	75	6.94	-17.4	73.9
1900-1910	90	13.61	20.0	96.1
1910-1920	138	34.76	53.3	155.4
1920-1930	149	45.16	8.0	29.9
1930-1940	112	57.89	-24.8	28.2
1940-1950	175	152.50	56.3	163.4
1950-1960	255	213.10	45.7	39.7
1960-1970	281	420.20	10.2	97.2
1970-1980	463	1135.10	64.8	170.1

*Each M2 is for the end of a decade. Thus .004 is M2 for 1770, and so on. Therefore, the money-growth rates of the last column are for each decade. For instance, the money-growth rate in the 1770s is give by

$$\frac{\text{M2 in 1780} - \text{M2 in 1770}}{\text{M2 in 1770}} \times 100 = \frac{.010 - .004}{.004} \times 100 = 150$$

AP_t = average WPI in decade t.

4

The Long-Run
Cycle of Inflation
in the United States

The previous chapter has demonstrated that the decennial rate of growth of money in the United States has followed an inexorable three-decade cycle at least since Independence, except during the convulsive times immediately following the Civil War. I have argued that this supports the concept of historical determinism and Sarkar's argument that the U.S. has been in the age of acquisitors ever since its birth. During this age, mainly the affluent and their wealth determine the behavior of major institutions in society including the economy, and since money constitutes the bulk of wealth in the modern age of acquisitors, the path of money growth is the primary determinant not only of economic health but also of many other social variables.

The fact that money growth in America has followed an exact cycle cresting every third decade implies that money indeed is the supreme nucleus under capitalism, for only a predominant entity can have an inexorable and stable cyclical path. How else could it be predominant and control the cycles of other variables?

The present chapter lends further credence to this hypothesis. Specifically, it is shown that the decennial rate of inflation in the United States has also followed a cyclical path that precisely parallels the long-run cycle of money growth. In other words, the rate of inflation per decade has also crested every third decade for over two centuries, except during the aftermath of the Civil War. This conclusion should not, of course, come as a surprise to Monetarists who picture a close association between money growth and inflation.

Developing the Long-run Cycle of Inflation

Inflation is generally defined as a state of persistent increase in general prices. A one-time rise in prices is not enough for the situation to be called inflationary.

Unlike the cycle of money growth, the cycle of inflation is not self-evident from the data on product prices. A simple averaging procedure is needed to obtain it.

Let us take a close look at the annual wholesale price index (WPI) in the United States. This index, thanks to Warren and Pearson, goes as far back as 1749, and is plotted in Chart 1. (The underlying data for this chart is presented in the appendix). The chart shows that there was not much change in wholesale prices in the United States from 1749 to 1939. Prices rose rapidly at times, but for almost 190 years they always came down shortly after reaching their peak. Since 1939, however, prices have moved only in one direction—upwards. The chart can thus be segmented into two parts: One, where prices move up and down, and the other where they rise and hardly ever decline. The chart tends to mask the continuity of U.S. inflation experience, as it appears that a discontinuity occurs around 1939. Until then the economy seems to have experienced regular cycles of inflation with prices periodically reaching their peak around 1780, 1810, 1865 and 1920, and then declining precipitously everytime. Even so, the chart reveals the rudiments of a long-run inflationary cycle, at least in 18th and 19th centuries

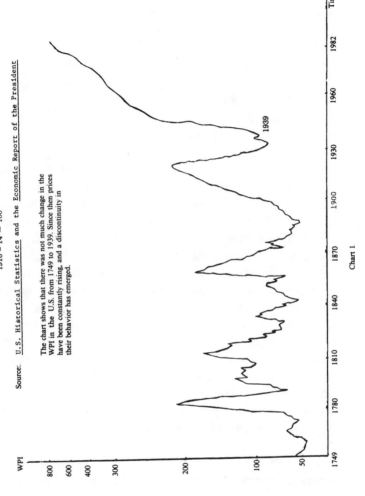

The Wholesale Price Index (WPI) in the United States (1749-1982)
1910 – 14 = 100

Source: U.S. Historical Statistics and the Economic Report of the President

The chart shows that there was not much change in the
WPI in the U.S. from 1749 to 1939. Since then prices
have been constantly rising, and a discontinuity in
their behavior has emerged.

1939

Chart 1.

Let us now transform the annual data of Chart 1 into decennial data. This is a common practice among economic historians who seek to identify trends underlying the long period of any time series. We can either add up annual prices to obtain the aggregate price level in each decade or take an arithmetic mean of prices per decade to obtain the average price level. Either statistic may represent the price level per decade. In this paper, we work with an average of the prices, but both procedures lead to exactly same results, because the average can be obtained by simply dividing the aggregate by eleven, which is taken as the number of years in a decade.

Consider Chart 2, which presents the average wholesale price level per decade and plots it against time. The first observation of this chart is the price level of 1749. Thus the price chart originates in that year, and assumes that the 1749 price represents the average price level of the 1740s. This assumption is clearly unnecessary, but gives us an extra observation, and helps with the visual appearance of the cycle developed later in Chart 3. Such a procedure is not without precedent, though. Kuznets often used it while converting his data into decade or five-yearly averages.

Chart 2 shows that the average price level per decade reached its periodic peaks in the 1780s, 1810s, 1860s, 1920s, and then declined for some time. This chart furnishes a somewhat better picture of the inflationary cycle than Chart 1 as annual price variations have been averaged out, yet the discontinuity in the price behavior remains. Here, following the decade of the 1930s, the average price level, unlike the case in preceding decades, rises continuously and never comes down. Thus, although the cycle of inflation is now relatively well-defined, it preserves the discontinuity observed in Chart 1.

But this discontinuity is more apparent than real. Let us transform the data of Chart 2 into rates of price change or inflation, and then plot them in Chart 3. There, the long-run cycle of inflation emerges as an eloquent testimony to

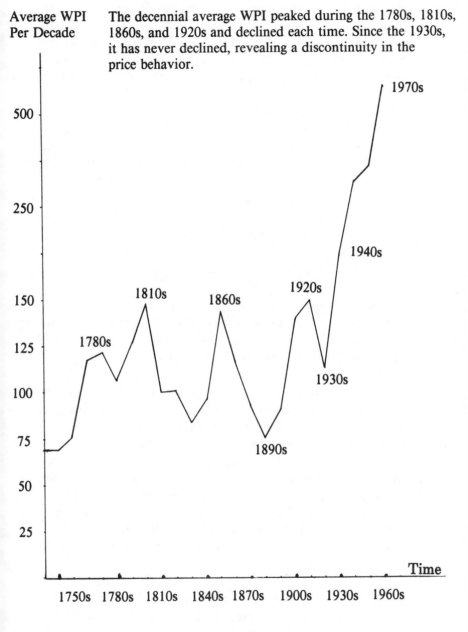

Decennial average wholesale price level with origin
at 1749 (1750-1980) 1910-14 = 100
Data Source: U.S. Historical Statistics

Average WPI
Per Decade

The decennial average WPI peaked during the 1780s, 1810s,
1860s, and 1920s and declined each time. Since the 1930s,
it has never declined, revealing a discontinuity in the
price behavior.

Chart 2

the resilience of the American economy. It is displayed by light and thin lines moving up and down through 23 decades, beginning with the decade of 1750s. Gone is the discontinuity of price behavior observed in earlier charts. Instead, as with the money-growth cycle of the previous chapter, a discontinuity appears following the 1860s—the decade of the Civil War.

Except for the post-Civil-War interregnum, Chart 3 displays an amazing phenomenon, namely that over the last 230 years the decennial rate of inflation reached its peak every third decade and then usually declined over the next two. Here the decennial rate of inflation is obtained in this way. For instance, for the 1970s, the inflation rate is given by,

$$\frac{\text{Average Price Level in 1970—Average Price Level in 1960}}{\text{Average Price Level in 1960}}$$

Another possibility is to define inflation by the proportionate change in prices within a decade, i.e., the decennial inflation rate could be obtained by dividing the difference between prices at the end and beginning of a decade by the beginning price. If prices were always rising, this perhaps would not be an improper procedure. But, as we have seen, for the major part of U.S. economic history, prices rose and fell within a decade, and also from decade to decade, in which case the difference between prices at the end and start of a decade could be highly misleading in that it might reveal price stability, whereas the average price level had in fact sharply risen above that in the previous decade. The procedure followed here not only uses all the data available for prices, but also applies to both cases where prices rise and fall and where they rise but do not fall.

In Chart 3 the first inflationary peak appears in the 1770s, following which the inflation rate declines over the next two decades and reaches another peak in the 1800s. Again it falls over the two subsequent decades, rising to its

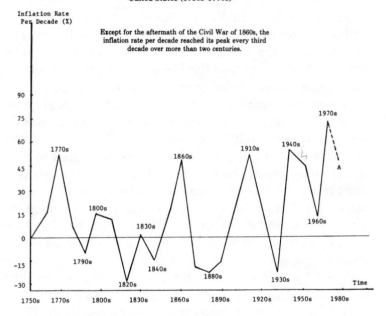

**The Long-Run Cycle of Inflation in the
United States (1750s–1770s)**

Except for the aftermath of the Civil War of 1860s, the
inflation rate per decade reached its peak every third
decade over more than two centuries.

Source: See the Appendix

Chart 3

81

zenith in the 1830s. This time the inflation rate declines only for one decade, but still the next peak appears thirty years later in the 1860s. At this point the decennial cycle is disturbed, but it begins anew with the 1880s, because within three decades the peak reappears in the 1910s, which is the first inflationary peak of the 20th century. Thirty years later, the cycle crests in the 1940s, and then again thirty years later in the 1970s. If we were to plot the inflation rates between 1980 and 1984 and if such rates were to continue in the rest of the 1980s, we would obtain a point such as A, showing that the 1970s were unmistakably the most recent peak of the decennial cycle of inflation.

A word may now be said for the inflationary peak of the 1830s. The peak appears virtually on the zero line. But the decades immediately preceding and following the 1830s reveal negative rates of inflation. Hence compared to these deflationary years, the zero rate of inflation represents at least relative inflation though not inflation in the absolute sense. Thus, it is not improper to regard the 1830s as the peak of the inflation (or deflation) cycle of the three decades between 1820 to 1850. Perhaps, a safer statement regarding the cycle during the 19th century is that the inflation peak following each trough occurred every third decade, excepting, of course, the two decades following the Civil War. Here the troughs of the cycle occur in the 1790s, 1820s, 1840s, 1880s, 1930s and 1960s, and except in the aftermath of the Civil War, each peak following the trough is spread at the interval of thirty years.

Inflation and Money Supply

What is the main cause of inflation? A great debate over this question occurred in the 1970s, but now a consensus has emerged among economists who believe that inflation springs chiefly from a prolonged monetary expansion. There may be other contributory factors, but they cannot sustain the spiral of rising prices in the absence of increasing growth in the supply of money. Thus a sustained

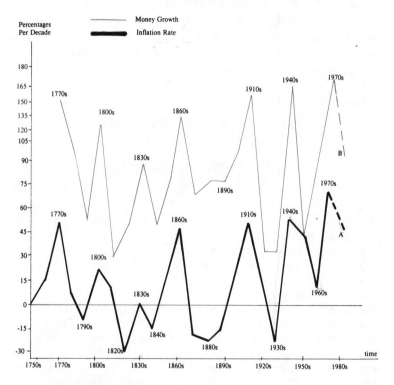

Long-Run Cycles of Inflation and Money Growth
Per Decade (1750s - 1970s)

Percentages
Per Decade

——— Money Growth
■■■■■■ Inflation Rate

Data sources (see the appendix)

Except for the aftermath of the Civil War of 1860s, the
money-growth rate per decade reached its peak every third
decade over more than two centuries, and so did the rate of
inflation.

Chart 4

rise in the growth of money is a prerequisite for the existence of inflation.

Chart 4 confirms this result in a resounding way. This chart presents the paths of money growth and inflation together and shows that the two cycles are almost parallel to each other. Not only do their peaks match, they are also both disturbed by the aftermath of the Civil War. This chart thus clearly reveals that money growth is the primary determinant of the rate of inflation: Every decade during which money growth crests is also the decade when the rate of inflation crests.

Data Appendix

The Wholesale Price Index (WPI)
In The United States

(1749-1983), 1910-14 = 100

Year	WPI	Year	WPI	Year	WPI	Year	WPI	Year	WPI
1749	68	1771	79	1793	102	1815	170	1837	115
1750	60	1772	89	1794	108	1816	151	1838	110
1751	65	1773	84	1795	131	1817	151	1839	112
1752	66	1774	76	1796	146	1818	147	1840	95
1753	65	1775	75	1797	131	1819	125	1841	92
1754	65	1776	86	1798	122	1820	106	1842	82
1755	66	1777	123	1799	126	1821	102	1843	75
1756	66	1778	140	1800	129	1822	106	1844	77
1757	65	1779	226	1801	142	1823	103	1845	83
1758	70	1780	225	1802	117	1824	98	1846	83
1759	79	1781	216	1803	118	1825	103	1847	90
1760	79	1782	175	1804	126	1826	99	1848	82
1761	77	1783	142	1805	141	1827	98	1849	82
1762	87	1784	115	1806	134	1828	97	1850	84
1763	79	1785	92	1807	130	1829	96	1851	83
1764	74	1786	90	1808	115	1830	91	1852	88
1765	72	1787	90	1809	130	1831	94	1853	97
1766	73	1788	90	1810	131	1832	95	1854	108
1767	77	1789	86	1811	•126	1833	95	1855	110
1768	74	1790	90	1812	131	1834	90	1856	105
1769	77	1791	85	1813	162	1835	100	1857	111
1770	77	1792	85	1814	182	1836	114	1858	93

Year	WPI	Year	WPI	Year	WPI	Year	WPI	Year	WPI
1859	95	1884	93	1909	99	1934	109	1959	269
1860	93	1885	85	1910	103	1935	117	1960	269
1861	89	1886	82	1911	95	1936	118	1961	268
1862	104	1887	85	1912	101	1937	126	1962	269
1863	133	1888	86	1913	102	1938	115	1963	268
1864	193	1889	81	1914	100	1939	113	1964	268
1865	185	1890	82	1915	101	1940	115	1965	274
1866	174	1891	82	1916	125	1941	128	1966	283
1867	162	1892	76	1917	172	1942	144	1967	283
1868	158	1893	78	1918	192	1943	151	1968	290
1869	151	1894	70	1919	202	1944	152	1969	302
1870	135	1895	71	1920	225	1945	155	1970	313
1871	130	1896	68	1921	142	1946	176	1971	323
1872	136	1897	68	1922	141	1947	217	1972	333
1873	133	1898	71	1923	147	1948	235	1973	363
1874	126	1899	76	1924	143	1949	223	1974	419
1875	118	1900	82	1925	151	1950	232	1975	464
1876	110	1901	81	1926	146	1951	258	1976	485
1877	106	1902	86	1927	140	1952	251	1977	516
1878	91	1903	87	1928	142	1953	248	1978	556
1879	90	1904	88	1929	139	1954	248	1979	618
1880	100	1905	88	1930	126	1955	249	1980	702
1881	103	1906	91	1931	107	1956	257	1981	766
1882	108	1907	95	1932	95	1957	264	1982	797
1883	101	1908	92	1933	96	1958	268	1983	810

The WPI data has been obtained as follows: For 1749-1970, see *Historical Statistics of the United States,* 1976 (series 52, pp. 201-2, and series 23, p. 199); for 1970-1983, see *Economic Report of the President,* 1984. Also see, Ravi Batra, *Renaissance Universal Journal,* Vol. 2-3, Fall 1984.

In series 52, 3 observations are missing for the years 1782 to 1784. This was the period immediately following the American revolution and prices were rapidly falling. The three missing observations were obtained by assuming that in each of these years prices fell at the same rate.

Similarly, figures were missing for 1788 and 1792, and since no trends are clear at these times, figures from the prior year were repeated for these years. For decennial average wholesale price index and inflation rates, which are based on the above table, see Table 1 in the appendix of Chapter 3.

5

The Long-Run
Cycle of Regulation
in the United States

It is now commonly recognized that main features of the economy during the 1970s were high inflation, high money growth and high regulation of business by the government. With the onset of the 1980s, all three have declined. Why? Is this phenomenon a mere coincidence or is it an integral part of certain trends in U.S. economy?

We have already seen that money growth and inflation move together in terms of a decennial cycle cresting every third decade. What about the degree of economic regulation by the government! Does it also move in tandem with the cycles already examined? The answer, surprisingly, turns out to be yes.

Many today believe that the 1970s experienced an unprecedented growth in federal regulation. Between 1970 and 1980, after all, twenty-one new regulatory agencies, with extensive powers to intervene in business decision-making of numerous industries, were established. The budget of the regulatory bodies expanded 600% during this period, while their staffing level grew by over 300%. Thus, the 1970s indeed experienced tremendous growth in the federal control over industry; yet this was not unprecedented. Tighter control had occurred during the

1940s when the economy was caught in the throes of the Second World War. The much-touted regulatory growth during the New Deal era of the 1930s actually pales before the one occurring during the next decade. Prior to that, in the 1910s also the economy had experienced a major surge in federal controls caused not only by the First World War but also by the preceding turmoil in financial markets.

A close study of U.S. economy reveals that the degree of regulation per decade has also followed a cyclical path similar to that of money growth and inflation explored before. It, too, has crested every third decade except during the trauma following the Civil War. Incredible as it may appear, this indeed turns out to be the case.

Regulation may be defined as government interference in the decision-making process of the private sector. Examples of such interference are minimum wage laws, standards for product quality, statutes against discrimination in labor-hiring, and so on. When a law is passed to regulate an industry, a federal agency is usually set up to oversee its activities. Hundreds of such agencies exist today. As of 1984 there were 138 regulatory bodies on the federal payroll.

One way to measure the degree of regulation in the economy then is to examine the new regulatory agencies established per decade. The higher is their number, the greater is the degree of regulation during those years. Another way is to look at the number of major economic laws passed by Congress. As such laws grow, state intervention in the economy increases. In this broader measure the regulation of business becomes synonymous with government interference with the operation of markets.

It may be noted that both these measures are compatible with an economy expanding over time. If the economy grows but regulatory bodies do not, then the degree of regulation per unit of production will decline or deregulation will occur. The same is true with major economic laws. In a growing economy, therefore, the proper measure of regulation (or deregulation) is the number of new regulatory agencies created or of new economic laws passed per decade. Credit for devising these indexes to quantify the degree of regulation, which is hard to measure, goes to Ronald Penoyer [23], who also provides us much of the relevant data presented in the appendix. To be sure, one should also consider any agencies abolished or any laws repealed. However, this seldom happens, and in what follows I examine only the new regulatory bodies established or the new economic measures passed per decade. As it turns out, this procedure, while simplifying the presentation, does not in any way invalidate my argument.

Consider Chart 1 which illustrates the time path of the two regulatory variables just described. Both of them can be seen to be following a rhythmical pattern. Cycle I displays the path of the new regulatory agencies established per decade, beginning with the 1830s. The first federal regulatory body was established in 1836, indicating that the 1830s constitute the first peak of this cycle. No agency was created in the 1840s and 1850s but two were legislated in the 1860s, so that the decade of the 1860s becomes another peak of the decennial regulatory cycle.

Following the Civil-War decade of 1860s, the cycle was disrupted, but resumed its normal path by cresting in the 1910s, 1940s and 1970s, where point A represents the new agencies created in the 1980s, assuming that the regulatory pace of the first four years of the Reagan administration is maintained through the rest of the decade. *Plot I shows that, except for the post-Civil-War interregnum, regulatory growth in the U.S. has followed an exact cycle, reaching a zenith every third decade.*

Although the first regulatory body was not established until the 1830s, this does not mean that regulation was absent until that time. Congress had passed many economic laws even before, with significant impact on the course of the economy. Data for this broader measure of regulation dates back to colonial times.

The time-path of major economic laws per decade is illustrated by Plot II, beginning with the 1760s. Here the first peak occurs in the 1770s, following which the economic legislation declines over the next two decades and crests again in the 1800s. Again it falls over the next two decades, rising to its zenith in the 1830s. This time the regulatory activity declines for only one decade, but still the subsequent peak occurs after 30 years in the 1860s, and so on. Again the 1910s, 1940s and 1970s are the peak decades of Plot II in the 20th century, with point B representing the number of major economic laws projected for the 1980s.

It may be noted that the first index of regulation, the one dealing with regulatory agencies, accords well with the fact that government control over the economy reached an all-time high during the 1940s when war-time regulations were introduced in almost every sector. Prices, interest, wages, rent and production were then controlled as never before nor ever since. Although during the 1940s, war was the main, if not the only, source of regulation, during the 1910s regulation soared not only because of the war, but also because of the preceding chaos in financial markets, a chaos leading to the creation of the Federal Reserve System in 1914. During the 1970s, by contrast, there was no war, but regulation peaked anyway. In other words, as with money growth and inflation, regulation tends to crest every third decade, but war is not its only cause.

A recurrent theme of this study is that since the United States has been in the age of acquisitors at least since its birth, wealth or money has been the primary determinant of most variables in society, not just the economy. The fact that the cycle of regulation is totally dictated by the cycle of money growth presented in Chapter 3 proves this hypothesis empirically. In other words, *throughout U.S. history, money or wealth was the nucleus around which*

THE LONG-RUN CYCLES OF REGULATORY GROWTH IN THE UNITED STATES (1760-1980).

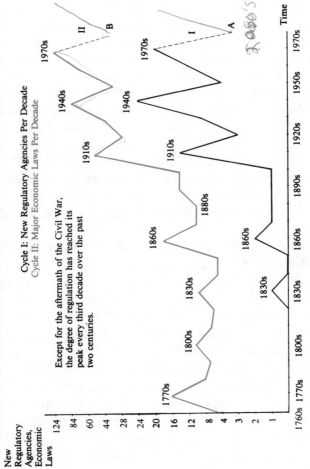

New Regulatory Agencies, Economic Laws

Cycle I: New Regulatory Agencies Per Decade
Cycle II: Major Economic Laws Per Decade

Except for the aftermath of the Civil War, the degree of regulation has reached its peak every third decade over the past two centuries.

Time

Chart 1

Sources: See the Appendix

revolved all social phenomena, including how the state governed its people.

It may be noted that since regulation peaks every third decade, deregulation also occurs at the same intervals of time. This is because deregulation signifies a decline in regulatory growth or an outright fall in regulation.

The chart of regulation does not reveal the full extent of deregulation that follows a war decade, because the economic laws passed to control the economy during the hostilities are abolished in peacetime. If this fact were taken into account, there might be negative regulatory growth in some decades if the economic laws repealed fell short of the ones enacted during the ten-year period. Chart 1, while compatible with the decline of regulation occurring after each war decade, fails to capture the full extent of this deregulation. Were this fact incorporated into the data, then each post-war decade, such as the 1780s, 1870s, 1920s, and 1950s, would turn out to be the peak decade of deregulation.

All this suggests that except for the disruption caused by the Civil War, the degree of deregulation has also peaked every third decade ever since the birth of the nation. In view of this, it is not surprising that the 1980s are witnessing an outright deregulation, not just an easing of regulation. Some regulatory bodies were actually abolished during the early 80s, while budgets and staffing of others were restrained. Between 1980 and 1985, airlines, trucking, banking, railroads, telecommunications, and oil and natural gas were partially or wholly deregulated, while two federal agencies, the Cost Accounting Standards Board and the Civil Aeronautics Board, were terminated. Hence the 1980s are likely to be another peak decade of deregulation.

Regulation, Inflation and Money

A comparison of Chart 1 with Chart 4 of the previous chapter reveals that the long-run cycle of regulation has followed exactly the same pattern as the long-run decennial cycles of money growth and inflation. Every regulatory peak is coinciding with the peak decades of inflation and money growth. And when the money-growth and inflation cycles are disrupted, as in the post-Civil-War period, the regulatory cycle is also disrupted. *This reasoning tends to suggest that inflation is not only a monetary phenomenon, it is also a regulatory phenomenon.* In other words, high money growth is only one cause of inflation. The economic inefficiency generated by increased regulation also contributes to it.

Is there any connection between the cycles of money growth and regulation? It is very hard to uncover a symbiotic relationship between the two variables. The explanation given by the law of social cycle is, of course, that in the age of acquisitors, wealth or money growth is the major determinant of all social activity. Yet the relationship between money growth and regulation is not altogether obvious. For the two variables are controlled by different branches of government. The Federal Reserve System (the Fed) controls the supply of money, whereas regulatory agencies are created by Congress.

One possible explanation is that the forces which stimulate the growth of money also generate the need for increased regulation by government. For instance, many peaks of money growth occurred during wars. The 1770s, 1860s, 1910s and 1940s were the decades during which the U.S. was caught in a major war, which had to be financed through the printing of money. But these wars also generated the need for government control over the economy, for private consumption had to be restrained to pave the way for increased defense production. Hence high money growth and a major expansion of regulatory agencies coincided in war decades, because in both cases the question of survival was at stake.

Similarly, the 1970s experienced a surge in both money supply and regulation. There was no war in this decade, but the forces underlying the growth of the two variables were the same.

Ever since the Keynesian revolution, the pro-interventionist sentiment among intellectuals has been rising. This sentiment reached its peak in the 1970s mainly because of the socio-economic problems created by an unprecedented rise in the price of oil. At the macro level, the pro-interventionist argument is simply that the government is responsible for a high level of employment, which has usually meant high money growth needed to finance expanding budget deficits. The same argument at the micro level is that the government is responsible for a clean environment, health and safety of workers, proper treatment of minorities by employers, anti-trust and anti-monopoly actions, and so on; and this spells further government regulation of business. Thus, in the 1970s there was no war, but the pro-interventionist sentiment was at its zenith. The result was a surge in both money growth and federal controls. History also reveals a high level of interventionist sentiment in the 1800s and 1830s, which were also peak decades of both money growth and regulation.

All this discussion suggests that the reason why both money growth and regulation crest together is that they are stimulated by the same set of exogenous forces such as war, pro-interventionist sentiment, etc.

With Reagan's election in 1980 and 1984, the interventionist attitude has declined. The free-market sentiment is now on the rise. Hence both money growth and the degree of regulation have fallen below their levels during the 1970s.

Current economic theory neglects the influence of regulation on inflation and focuses mainly on the annual rate of money growth. Monetarism has won over the experts, at least as far as the question of inflation is concerned. Anytime the Fed announces that money has been growing above its recent average, forecasts come pouring about the resurgence of inflation. This obsession with money has led to faulty predictions from prominent scholars, including Milton Friedman. In an article in the *Wall Street Journal* (December 10, 1984, p. 20), Clark and McGinley conclude that "late last year, Milton Friedman predicted a recession in the first half of 1984 and soaring inflation in the second half. *He was dead wrong:* The economy boomed in the first half, and there aren't any indications of a major recession in the second." (My italics).

The reason why inflation is not rising with rising money growth at present is that major deregulation is now under way. Deregulation promotes a competitive environment in which businessmen find it difficult to raise prices at will. Nor can labor unions win inflationary wage increases. Besides, the long-run decennial cycle of inflation is now in its downswing, but the experts have failed to recognize this trend. That is why, I think that even their long-run forecasts will be wrong. Ralph Winter reports "that the consensus forecast of a group of 47 leading economists . . . is for a 5.3% annual rise in the consumer price index for 1985-89 and a slightly lower 5.1% yearly rise from 1990 through 1994." (*Wall Street Journal,* December 11, 1984, p. 24).

This forecast is inconsistent with the long-run cycle of inflation. In my view, the annual rate of inflation during the 1980s will hover around 4.5%, and the 1990s will experience deflation, which means negative inflation. Between 1990 and 1994, prices will actually fall. All this is explained in the next chapter.

Before concluding this chapter, a word may be said about the merits of the Penoyer indexes of regulation. Clearly, the two indexes are not fool-proof. But they do conform with some indisputable facts about regulatory activity occurring in U.S. annals. It is well known that federal control over the economy surged during the 1970s, 1940s, 1910s, 1860s and 1770s, but declined during the

1920s, 1950s and so far in the 1980s. The regulatory cycles based on the Penoyer indexes do not conflict with such incontrovertible facts. In other words, although the two regulatory measures are far from perfect, they do yield invaluable information supporting the hypothesis of historical determinism.

Data Appendix

Table 1

Chronology of Major Regulatory Bodies

1830-1840

    1.   Patent and Trademark Office, 1836

1840-1850

    None

1850-1860

    None

1860-1870

    1.   Comptroller of the Currency, 1863
    2.   Copyright Office, 1870

1870-1880

    1.   Copyright Office, 1870

1880-1890

    1.   Interstate Commerce Commission, 1887

1890-1900

    1.   Army Corps of Engineers, 1899

1900-1910

    1.   Antitrust Division, 1903

1910-1920

    1.   Federal Reserve System (Board of Governors), 1913
    2.   Federal Trade Commission, 1914
    3.   Coast Guard, 1915
    4.   Tariff Commission, 1916
    5.   Federal Power Commission, 1920

In addition to these agencies, the following major regulatory bodies were set up during the 1910s for the sake of successful prosecution of the First World War that began in 1914.

    6.   Council of National Defense, 1916

7. Shipping Board, 1916
8. Food Administration, 1917
9. Fuel Administration, 1917
10. Railroad Administration, 1917
11. War Industries Board, 1917
12. War Trade Board, 1917
13. War Finance Corporation, 1918
14. Labor Administration, 1918

1920-1930

1. Federal Power Commission, 1920
2. Commodity Exchange Authority, 1922
3. Bureau of Customs, 1927

1930-1940

1. Food and Drug Administration, 1931
2. Federal Home Loan Bank Board, 1932
3. Farm Credit Administration, 1933
4. Federal Deposit Insurance Corporation, 1933
5. Federal Communications Commission, 1934
6. Securities and Exchange Commission, 1934
7. National Labor Relations Board, 1935
8. Maritime Administration, 1936
9. Agricultural Marketing Service and Other Agencies, 1937
10. Civil Aeronautics Authority, 1938
11. Fish and Wildlife Service, 1940

1940-1950

1. Fish and Wildlife Service, 1940
2. Atomic Energy Commission, 1946

In addition to these agencies, the following major regulatory bodies were established during the 1940s to successfully prosecute the Second World War in which the U.S. was involved, one way or another, from 1940 to 1946.

3. Board of Economic Warfare
4. Food Distribution Administration
5. Food Production Administration
6. Foreign Economic Administration
7. National Defense Advisory Commission
8. National Housing Agency
9. National Wage Stabilization Board
10. National War Labor Board
11. Office for Emergency Management
12. Office of Economic Stabilization
13. Office of Economic Warfare
14. Office of Export Control
15. Office of Petroleum Coordinator for National Defense
16. Office of Price Administration
17. Office of Produce Management
18. Retraining and Reemployment Administration
19. Surplus Property Administration
20. Wage Adjustment Board for the Construction Industry
21. War Insurance Corporation

Cycle of Regulation

22. War Manpower Commission
23. War Production Board
24. War Shipping Administration

1950-1960

1. Renegotiation Board, 1951
2. Foreign Agricultural Service, 1953
3. Small Business Administration, 1953
4. Federal Aviation Agency, 1958

1960-1970

1. Agricultural Stabilization and Conservation Service, 1961
2. Labor-Management Services Administration, 1963
3. Equal Employment Opportunity Commission, 1964
4. Federal Highway Administration, 1966
5. National Transportation Safety Board, 1966
6. Federal Railroad Administration, 1966
7. Council on Environmental Quality, 1969
8. Cost Accounting Standards Board, 1970
9. Environmental Protection Agency, 1970
10. National Credit Union Administration, 1970
11. National Highway Traffic Safety Administration, 1970
12. Occupational Safety and Health Administration, 1970

1970-1980

1. Cost Accounting Standards Board, 1970
2. Environmental Protection Agency, 1970
3. National Credit Union Administration, 1970
4. National Highway Traffic Safety Administration, 1970
5. Occupational Safety and Health Administration, 1970
6. Employment Standards Administration, 1971
7. Occupational Safety and Health Review Commission, 1971
8. Bureau of Alcohol, Tobacco, and Firearms, 1972
9. Consumer Product Safety Commission, 1972
10. Domestic and International Business Administration, 1972
11. Drug Enforcement Administration, 1973
12. Federal Energy Administration, 1973
13. Mining Enforcement and Safety Administration, 1973
14. Council on Wage and Price Stability, 1974
15. Federal Election Commission, 1975
16. Materials Transportation Bureau, 1975
17. Federal Grain Inspection Service, 1975
18. Office of Neighborhoods, Voluntary Associations, and Consumer Protection, 1977
19. Office of Surface Mining Reclamation and Enforcement, 1977
20. Office of the Federal Inspector of the Alaska Natural Gas Transportation System, 1979

1980-1984

1. Packers and Stockyards Administration, Department of Agriculture, 1982

Table 2

Regulatory Legislation per Decade

1760-1770

1. Sugar Act, 1764
2. Prohibition against printing paper money, 1764
3. Stamp Act, 1765
4. Townshend Revenue Act, 1767

1770-1780

1. Tea Act, 1773
2. Coercive or Intolerable Acts, 1774
3. Bill to appoint a Treasurer, 1775
4. Funding Act, 1775
5. Bill to strengthen the treasury, 1776
6. Funding Act, 1776
7. Bill to open American ports to all nations except England, 1776
8. Bill to establish an Office of Accounts, 1776
9. Funding Act, 1777
10. Bill to appoint Loan Commissioners, 1777
11. Bill to appoint Boards of Treasury, 1778
12. Funding Act, 1778
13. Bill to have a commercial agreement with France, 1778
14. Bill to strengthen the Boards of Treasury, 1779
15. Funding Act, 1779
16. Law regarding specie value of currency, 1780

1780-1790

1. Law regarding specie value of currency, 1780
2. Law regarding specie value of currency, 1781
3. Bank of North America Act, 1781
4. Law establishing the Office of Superintendent of Finance, 1781
5. Land Ordinance, 1784
6. Land Ordinance, 1785
7. Land Ordinance, 1786
8. Funding Act, 1790

1790-1800

1. Funding Act, 1790
2. Whiskey Tax Act, 1791
3. First United States Bank Act, 1791
4. Tariff Act, 1792
5. Revenue Act, 1794
6. Land Act, 1796
7. Land Act, 1800

1800-1810

1. Land Act, 1800
2. Revenue Act, 1802
3. Tariff Act, 1804

4. Land Act, 1804
5. National Turnpike Act, 1806
6. Debt Conversion Act, 1807
7. Slave Importation Law, 1807
8. Tariff Act, 1807
9. Embargo Act, 1807
10. Non-intercourse Act, 1809

1810-1820

1. Tariff Act, 1812
2. Revenue Act, 1813
3. Second United States Bank Act, 1816
4. Tariff Act, 1816
5. Tariff Act, 1818
6. Land Act, 1819
7. Land Act, 1820

1820-1830

1. Land Act, 1820
2. Pension Act, 1823
3. Tariff Act, 1824
4. Tariff Act, 1828
5. Preemption Act, 1830
6. Tariff Act, 1830

1830-1840

1. Preemption Act, 1830
2. Tariff Act, 1830
3. Tariff Act, 1832
4. Tariff Act, 1833
5. Coinage Act, 1834
6. Deposit Act, 1836
7. Patent Act, 1836
8. Act requiring federal inspection of steamboats, 1836
9. Independent Treasury Bill, 1840

1840-1850

1. Independent Treasury Bill, 1840
2. Preemption Act, 1841
3. Tariff Act, 1842
4. Independent Treasury Bill, 1846
5. Tariff Act, 1846

1850-1860

1. Coinage Act, 1853
2. Kansas-Nebraska Act, 1854
3. Graduation Act, 1854
4. Tariff Act, 1857
5. Independent Treasury Act, 1857

1860-1870

1. Morrill Tariff Act, 1861
2. Loan Act, 1861

3.   Tax Act, 1861
4.   Morrill Land Grant Act, 1862
5.   Revenue Act, 1862
6.   Homestead Act, 1862
7.   Tariff Act, 1862
8.   Pacific Railway Act, 1862
9.   Tariff Act, 1863
10.   National Bank Act, 1863
11.   Currency Act, 1863
12.   Revenue Act, 1863
13.   National Bank Act, 1864
14.   Revenue Act, 1864
15.   Revenue Act, 1865
16.   Funding Act, 1866
17.   Refunding Act, 1870
18.   Copyright Act, 1870

1870-1880

1.   Refunding Act, 1870
2.   Copyright Act, 1870
3.   Tariff Act, 1873
4.   Coinage Act, 1873
5.   Timber Culture Act, 1873
6.   Tariff Act, 1875
7.   Desert-Land Act, 1877
8.   Timber and Stone Act, 1878
9.   Bland-Allison Act, 1878
10.   Pension-Arrears Act, 1879

1880-1890

1.   Immigration Act, 1882
2.   Tariff Act, 1883
3.   Hatch Act, 1883
4.   Law regarding animal and plant health inspection, 1884
5.   Interstate Commerce Act, 1887
6.   Sherman Silver Purchase Act, 1890
7.   Sherman Anti-Trust Act, 1890
8.   McKinley Tariff Act, 1890
9.   Morrill Act, 1890
10.   Law regarding importation of certain animals, 1890

1890-1900

1.   Sherman Silver Purchase Act, 1890
2.   Sherman Anti-Trust Act, 1890
3.   McKinley Tariff Act, 1890
4.   Morrill Act, 1890
5.   Law regarding importation of certain animals, 1890
6.   Forest Reserve Act, 1891
7.   Wilson-Gorman Act, 1894
8.   Dockery Act, 1894
9.   Dingley Tariff, 1897
10.   Tea Importation Act, 1897
11.   River and Harbor Act, 1899

12. Currency Act, 1900
13. Gold Standard Act, 1900
14. Lacey Act, 1900

1900-1910

1. Currency Act, 1900
2. Gold Standard Act, 1900
3. Lacey Act, 1900
4. Law regarding animal and plant health inspection, 1903
5. Elkins Act, 1903
6. Expediting Act, 1903
7. Law regarding animal and plant health inspection, 1905
8. Law regarding dredged material dumping, 1905
9. Pure Food and Drug Act, 1906
10. Hepburn Act, 1906
11. Copyright Act, 1909
12. Payne-Aldrich Act, 1909
13. Mine Safety Act, 1910
14. Mann-Elkins Act, 1910

1910-1920

1. Mine Safety Act, 1910
2. Mann-Elkins Act, 1910
3. Plant Quarantine Act, 1912
4. Panama Canal Act, 1912
5. Income-Tax Act, 1913
6. Underwood Tariff Act, 1913
7. Federal Reserve Act, 1913
8. Clayton Act, 1914
9. Federal Trade Commission Act, 1914
10. Coast Guard Act, 1915
11. Adamson Act, 1916
12. Shipping Act, 1916
13. Highway Act, 1916
14. National Defense Act, 1916
15. U.S. Warehouse Act, 1916
16. Federal Employee Compensation Act, 1916
17. Federal Farm Loan Act, 1916
18. Each Car Service Act, 1917
19. Liberty Loan Act, 1917
20. Lever Food and Fuel Control Act, 1917
21. Law regarding danger zones in navigable waters, 1918
22. Pittman Act, 1918
23. Migratory Bird Treaty Act, 1918
24. Jones Act, 1920
25. Esch-Cummins Transportation Act, 1920
26. Water Power Act, 1920
27. Mineral Lands Leasing Act, 1920
28. Merchant Marine Act, 1920

In addition to the above laws, the following regulatory actions or acts relate to the successful prosecution of the war effort during the 1910s:

29.   Council of National Defense, 1916
30.   National Research Council, 1918
31.   Board of Inventions, 1917
32.   Trading-with-the-enemy Act, 1917
33.   War Finance Corporation Act, 1918
34.   Committee on Coal Production, 1917
35.   Agricultural Production Stimulation Act, 1917
36.   Fuel Production Act, 1917
37.   Aircraft Board, 1917
38.   American Relief Administration, 1919
39.   Board of Control of Labor Standards in Army Clothing, 1917
40.   Board of Mediation and Conciliation, 1913
41.   Board of Railway Wages and Working Conditions, 1918
42.   Bureau of Industrial Housing and Transportation, 1918
43.   Bureau of War Risk Insurance, 1914
44.   Commercial Economy Board, 1917
45.   Emergency Fleet Corporation, 1917
46.   Food Administration, 1917
47.   National Research Council, 1918
48.   Labor Administration, 1918
49.   Munitions Standards Board, 1917
50.   National Adjustment Commission, 1917
51.   Railroad Administration, 1917
52.   Shipping Board, 1916
53.   Sugar Equalization Board, 1918
54.   War Credits Board, 1917
55.   War Industries Board, 1917
56.   War Labor Policies Board, 1918
57.   War Trade Board, 1917

1920-1930

1.   Jones Act, 1920
2.   Esch-Cummins Transportation Act, 1920
3.   Water Power Act, 1920
4.   Mineral Lands Leasing Act, 1920
5.   Merchant Marine Act, 1920
6.   Emergency Tariff Act, 1921
7.   Revenue Act, 1921
8.   Anti-Trust Exemption Law, 1921
9.   Anti-Dumping Act, 1921
10.   Packers and Stockyards Act, 1921
11.   Immigration Act, 1921
12.   Budget and Accounting Act, 1921
13.   Fordney-McCumber Act, 1922
14.   Commodity Exchange Act, 1922
15.   Filled Milk Act, 1923
16.   Intermediate Credits Act, 1923
17.   Revenue Act, 1924
18.   Capper-Volstead Act, 1926
19.   Black Bass Act, 1926
20.   Revenue Act, 1926
21.   Railroad Labor Act, 1926
22.   Produce Act, 1927

23.   Customs Bureau Act, 1927
24.   Longshoremen's and Harbor Worker's Compensation Act, 1927
25.   McFaden Branch Banking Act, 1927
26.   Jones-White Act, 1928
27.   Revenue Act, 1928
28.   Migratory Bird Act, 1929
29.   Agricultural Marketing Act, 1929
30.   Smoot-Hawley Tariff Act, 1930
31.   Perishable Agricultural Act, 1930

1930-1940

1.   Smoot-Hawley Tariff Act, 1930
2.   Perishable Agricultural Act, 1930
3.   Agricultural Appropriations Act, 1931
4.   Animal Damage Control Act, 1931
5.   Davis-Bacon Act, 1931
6.   Federal Home Loan Bank Act, 1932
7.   Federal Reserve Act, 1933
8.   Home Owners Loan Act, 1933
9.   Securities Act, 1933
10.   Banking Act, 1933
11.   Agriculture Adjustment Act, 1933
12.   Intercoastal Shipping Act, 1933
13.   Securities Exchange Act, 1934
14.   Communications Act, 1934
15.   Federal Credit Union Act, 1934
16.   National Housing Act, 1934
17.   Fish and Wildlife Coordination Act, 1934
18.   Migratory Bird Hunting Stamp Act, 1934
19.   Gold Reserve Act, 1934
20.   Soil Conservation and Domestic Allotments Act, 1935
21.   Anti-Smuggling Act, 1935
22.   Tobacco Inspection Act, 1935
23.   Federal Alcohol Administration Act, 1935
24.   National Labor Relations Act, 1935
25.   Federal Power Act, 1935
26.   Banking Act, 1935
27.   Motor Carrier Act, 1935
28.   Public Utility Holding Company Act, 1935
29.   Robinson-Patman Act, 1936
30.   Public Contracts Act, 1936
31.   Liquor Enforcement Act, 1936
32.   Law Regarding North Atlantic Vessel Operators, 1936
33.   Agricultural Marketing Agreement Act, 1937
34.   Federal Aid in Wildlife Restoration Act, 1937
35.   Bankruptcy Act, 1938
36.   Civil Aeronautics Act, 1938
37.   Natural Gas Act, 1938
38.   Fair Labor Standard Acts, 1938
39.   Agricultural Adjustment Act, 1938
40.   Food, Drug and Cosmetic Act, 1938
41.   Federal Seed Act, 1939
42.   Trust Indenture Act, 1939
43.   Investment Company Act, 1940

44.	Investment Advisers Act, 1940
45.	Wool Products Labelling Act, 1940
46.	Bald Eagle Protection Act, 1940
47.	Reorganization Plan No. 3, 1940
48.	Motorboat Act, 1940

1940-1950

1.	Investment Company Act, 1940
2.	Investment Advisers Act, 1940
3.	Wool Products Labelling Act, 1940
4.	Bald Eagle Protection Act, 1940
5.	Reorganization Plan No. 3, 1940
6.	Motorboat Act, 1940
7.	Organic Act, 1944
8.	Public Health Services Act, 1944
9.	Administrative Procedure Act, 1946
10.	Agricultural Marketing Act, 1946
11.	Atomic Energy Act, 1946
12.	Lanham Trademark Act, 1946
13.	Law regarding Animal and Plant Health Inspection, 1947
14.	Labor-Management Relations Act, 1947
15.	Explosives and Dangerous Articles Act, 1948
16.	Reed-Bullwinkle Act, 1948
17.	Export Control Act, 1949
18.	First Revenue Act, 1950
19.	Celler-Kefauver Act, 1950
20.	Defense Production Act, 1950
21.	Federal Deposit Insurance Act, 1950
22.	Federal Aid in Fish Restoration Act, 1950

In addition to the regulatory laws mentioned above, the following agencies were established during the 1940s by Executive Orders of the President to regulate the economy in the interest of victory in war. These executive orders had the same force as any economic legislation passed by Congress.

23.	Advisory Board on Just Compensation
24.	Board of Economic Warfare
25.	Civilian Production Administration
26.	Coal Mines Administrator
27.	Colonial Mica Corporation
28.	Combined Food Board
29.	Combined Production and Resources Board
30.	Combined Raw Materials Board
31.	Combined Shipping Adjustment Board
32.	Defense Plant Corporation
33.	Defense Supplies Corporation
34.	Food Distribution Administration
35.	Food Production Administration
36.	Foreign Economic Administration
37.	Foreign Funds Control
38.	National Defense Advisory Commission
39.	National Defense Mediation Board
40.	National Housing Agency
41.	National Mediation Board

42.	National Wage Stabilization Board
43.	National War Labor Board
44.	Office for Coordination of National Defense Purchases
45.	Office for Emergency Management
46.	Office of Agricultural Defense Relations
47.	Office of Contract Settlement
48.	Office of Defense Health and Welfare Service
49.	Office of Defense Transportation
50.	Office of Economic Stabilization
51.	Office of Economic Warfare
52.	Office of Export Control
53.	Office of Fishery Coordination
54.	Office of Merchant Ship Control
55.	Office of Petroleum Coordinator for National Defense
56.	Office of Price Administration
57.	Office of Production Management
58.	Office of Production Research and Development
59.	Office of Scientific Research and Development
60.	Petroleum Administration for War
61.	Priorities Board
62.	Reconstruction Finance Corporation
63.	Retraining and Reemployment Administration
64.	Rubber Development Corporation
65.	Smaller War Plants Corporation
66.	Southwestern Power Administration
67.	Steel Recovery Corporation
68.	Surplus Property Administration
69.	U.S. Commercial Company
70.	Wage Adjustment Board for the Construction Industry
71.	War Assets Corporation
72.	War Contracts Price Adjustment Board
73.	War Food Administration
74.	War Hemp Industries
75.	War Insurance Corporation
76.	War Manpower Commission
77.	War Production Board
78.	War Resources Board
79.	War Shipping Administration
80.	War Resources Council

1950-1960

1.	Defense Production Act, 1950
2.	Federal Deposit Insurance Corporation, 1950
3.	Federal Aid in Fish Restoration Act, 1950
4.	First Revenue Act, 1950
5.	Second Revenue Act, 1950
6.	Celler-Kefauver Act, 1950
7.	Revenue Act, 1951
8.	Taft-Humphrey Act, 1951
9.	Renegotiation Act, 1951
10.	Fur Products Labelling Act, 1951
11.	Patent Act, 1952
12.	McGuire Keogh Act, 1952
13.	Small Business Act, 1953

14. Reorganization Plan No. 2, 1953
15. Outer Continental Shelf Lands Act, 1953
16. Agricultural Act, 1954
17. Atomic Energy Act, 1954
18. Flammable Fabrics Act, 1954
19. Internal Revenue Code, 1954
20. Housing Act, 1954
21. Anti-Trust Improvement Act, 1955
22. Federal Home Loan Act, 1955
23. Bank Holding Company Act, 1956
24. Fish and Wildlife Act, 1956
25. Fair-Labor Standards Act, 1956
26. Guidelines for Inspection of Passenger Vessels, 1956
27. Refrigerator Safety Act, 1956
28. Federal Plant Pests Act, 1957
29. Poultry Products Inspection Act, 1957
30. Federal Aviation Act, 1958
31. Teller Act, 1958
32. Humane Slaughter Act, 1958
33. Food Additives Amendment, 1958
34. Small Business Act, 1958
35. Small Business Investment Act, 1958
36. Textile Fiber Products Identification Act, 1958
37. Landrum-Griffin Act, 1959
38. Bank Merger Act, 1960
39. Great Lakes Pilotage Act, 1960
40. Hazardous Substances Act, 1960
41. Color Additives Amendments, 1960

1960-1970

1. Great Lakes Pilotage Act, 1960
2. Hazardous Substances Act, 1960
3. Color Additives Amendments, 1960
4. Bank Merger Act, 1960
5. Act of September 6, 1961
6. Oil Pollution Act, 1961
7. Wetlands, Act, 1961
8. Act of July 2, 1962
9. Drug Amendments Act, 1962
10. Refuge Recreation Act, 1962
11. Bank Service Corporation Act, 1962
12. Communications Satellite Act, 1962
13. Trade Expansion Act, 1962
14. Equal Pay Act, 1963
15. Farm Labor Contractor Registration Act, 1963
16. Civil Rights Act, 1964
17. Meat Import Act, 1964
18. Highway Beautification Act, 1965
19. Executive Order, 1965
20. Service Contract Act, 1965
21. Anadromous Fish Conservation Act, 1965
22. Public Works and Economic Development Act, 1965
23. Federal Laboratory Animal Welfare Act, 1966

Cycle of Regulation

24. National Traffic and Motor Vehicle Safety Act, 1966
25. Highway Safety Act, 1966
26. Department of Transportation Act, 1966
27. Fair Packaging and Labelling Act, 1966
28. Federal Hazardous Substances Act, 1966
29. Federal Metal and Non-metallic Mine Safety Act, 1966
30. Public Law 89-777, 1966
31. Department of Transportation Act, 1966
32. Clean Air Act, 1967
33. Federal Meat Inspection Act, 1967
34. Age Discrimination in Employment Act, 1967
35. Agricultural Fair Practices Act, 1968
36. Omnibus Crime Control and Safe Streets Act, 1968
37. Interstate Land Sales Full Disclosure Act, 1968
38. Radiation Control for Health and Safety Act, 1968
39. Gun Control Act, 1968
40. Consumer Credit Protection Act, 1968
41. Open Housing Act, 1968
42. Truth-in-Lending Act, 1968
43. Bank Protection Act, 1968
44. Public Law 90-298, 1968
45. Federal Coal Mine Health and Safety Act, 1969
46. Construction Safety Act, 1969
47. National Wildlife Refuge System Administration Act, 1969
48. National Environmental Policy Act, 1969
49. Natural Gas Pipeline Safety Act, 1969
50. Export Administration Act, 1969
51. Wheat Research and Promotion Act, 1970
52. Airport and Airway Revenue Act, 1970
53. Organized Crime Control Act, 1970
54. Rail Passenger Service Act, 1970
55. Federal Railroad Safety Act, 1970
56. Comprehensive Drug Abuse Prevention and Control Act, 1970
57. Horse Protection Act, 1970
58. Water Bank Act, 1970
59. Plant Variety Protection Act, 1970
60. Egg Products Inspection Act, 1970
61. Poison Prevention Packaging Act, 1970
62. Highway Safety Act, 1970
63. Occupational Safety and Health Act, 1970
64. National Environmental Improvement Act, 1970
65. Reorganization Plan No. 3, 1970
66. Reorganization Plan No. 4, 1970
67. Water Quality Improvement Act, 1970
68. National Credit Union Administration Act, 1970
69. Home Finance Act, 1970
70. National Credit Union Share Insurance Act, 1970
71. Bank Records and Foreign Transactions Act, 1970
72. Fair Credit Reporting Act, 1970
73. Disaster Relief Act, 1970

Data Appendix

1970-1980

1. Wheat Research and Promotion Act, 1970
2. Airport and Airway Revenue Act, 1970
3. Organized Crime Control Act, 1970
4. Rail Passenger Service Act, 1970
5. Federal Railroad Safety Act, 1970
6. Comprehensive Drug Abuse Prevention and Control Act, 1970
7. Horse Protection Act, 1970
8. Water Bank Act, 1970
9. Plant Variety Protection Act, 1970
10. Egg Products Inspection Act, 1970
11. Poison Prevention Packaging Act, 1970
12. Highway Safety Act, 1970
13. Occupational Safety and Health Act, 1970
14. National Environmental Improvement Act, 1970
15. Reorganization Plan No. 3, 1970
16. Reorganization Plan No. 4, 1970
17. Water Quality Improvement Act, 1970
18. National Credit Union Administration Act, 1970
19. Home Finance Act, 1970
20. National Credit Union Share Insurance Act, 1970
21. Bank Records and Foreign Transactions Act, 1970
22. Fair Credit Reporting Act, 1970
23. Disaster Relief Act, 1970
24. Federal Boat Safety Act, 1971
25. Lead-Based Paint Poisoning Prevention Act, 1971
26. Postal Reorganization Act, 1971
27. Alaska Native Claims Settlement Act, 1971
28. Farm Credit Act, 1971
29. Ports and Waterways Safety Act, 1972
30. Federal Water Pollution Control Act Amendments, 1972
31. Motor Vehicle Information and Cost Saving Act, 1972
32. Consumer Product Safety Act, 1972
33. Equal Employment Opportunity Act, 1972
34. Federal Insecticide, Fungicide, and Rodenticide Act, 1972
35. Marine Mammal Protection Act, 1972
36. Noise Control Act, 1972
37. Coastal Zone Management Act, 1972
38. Marine Protection, Research, and Sanctuaries Act, 1972
39. Public Law 91-416, 1972
40. Reorganization Plan No. 2, 1973
41. Federal Aid Highway Act, 1973
42. Regional Rail Reorganization Act, 1973
43. Rehabilitation Act, 1973
44. Endangered Species Act, 1973
45. Emergency Petroleum Allocation Act, 1973
46. NOW Accounts Act, 1973
47. Trans-Alaska Pipeline Authorization Act, 1973
48. Consolidated Farm and Rural Development Act, 1973
49. Narcotic Addict Treatment Act, 1974
50. National Mobile Home Construction and Safety Standards Act, 1974
51. Real Estate Settlement Procedures Act, 1974
52. Trade Act, 1974

53. Deepwater Port Act, 1974
54. Independent Safety Board Act, 1974
55. Health Care Institutions Act, 1974
56. Employee Retirement Income Security Act, 1974
57. Vietnam Era Veterans Readjustment Assistance Act, 1974
58. Federal Energy Act, 1974
59. Federal Energy Administration Act, 1974
60. Energy Supply and Environmental Coordination Act, 1974
61. Energy Reorganization Act, 1974
62. Safe Drinking Water Act, 1974
63. Fair Credit Billing Act, 1974
64. Equal Credit Opportunity Act, 1974
65. Act of October 23, 1974
66. Trade Expansion Act, 1974
67. Council on Wage and Price Stability Act, 1974
68. Federal Election Campaign Act Amendments of 1974
69. Hazardous Material Transportation Act, 1975
70. Energy Policy and Conservation Act, 1975
71. Home Mortgage Disclosure Act, 1975
72. Magnuson-Moss Warranty Federal Trade Commission Improvement Act, 1975
73. Railroad Revitalization and Regulatory Reform Act, 1976
74. Medical Devices Amendments, 1976
75. International Security Assistance and Arms Control Act, 1976
76. Airport and Airway Development Act Amendments, 1976
77. Hart-Scott-Rodino Antitrust Improvement Act, 1976
78. Crime Control Act, 1976
79. U.S. Grain Standards Act, 1976
80. Energy Conservation and Production Act, 1976
81. Toxic Substances Control Act, 1976
82. Resource Conservation and Recovery Act, 1976
83. Consumer Leasing Act, 1976
84. Act of October 19, 1976
85. Food and Agriculture Act, 1977
86. Federal Mine Safety and Health Amendments Act, 1977
87. Black Lung Benefits Reform Act, 1977
88. Department of Energy Organization Act, 1977
89. Clean Water Act, 1977
90. Surface Mining Control and Reclamation Act, 1977
91. Fair Debt Collection Practices Act, 1977
92. Housing and Community Development Act, 1977
93. Community Reinvestment Act, 1977
94. Treasury Department Order No. 120-1, 1978
95. Neighborhood Self-Help Development Act, 1978
96. Liveable Cities Act, 1978
97. Customs Procedural Reform and Simplification Act, 1978
98. Trafficking in Contraband Cigarettes Act, 1978
99. Reorganization Plan No. 1, 1978
100. Pregnancy Discrimination Act, 1978
101. Civil Service Reform Act, 1978
102. Antarctic Conservation Act, 1978
103. Power Plant and Industrial Fuel Use Act, 1978
104. International Banking Act, 1978

105.	Financial Institutions Regulatory and Interest Rate Control Act, 1978
106.	National Credit Union Administration Central Liquidity Facility Act, 1978
107.	Outer Continental Shelf Lands Act Amendments, 1978
108.	Act of September 30, 1978
109.	Airline Deregulation Act, 1978
110.	Cargo Deregulation Act, 1978
111.	Natural Gas Policy Act, 1978
112.	Trade Agreements Act, 1979
113.	Hazardous Liquid Pipeline Safety Act, 1979
114.	Reorganization Plan No. 1, Executive Order No. 12142, 1979
115.	Aviation Safety and Noise Abatement Act, 1979
116.	International Air Transportation Act, 1979
117.	Reorganization Plan No. 3, 1979
118.	Federal Election Campaign Act Amendments, 1979
119.	Export Administration Act, 1979
120.	Crude Oil Windfall Profits Act, 1980
121.	Comprehensive Environmental Response, Compensation and Liability Act, 1980
122.	Depository Institutions Deregulation and Monetary Control Act, 1980
123.	Motor Carrier Act, 1980
124.	Staggers Rail Act, 1980
125.	Federal Trade Commission Improvement Act, 1980

Table 1 has been compiled from Penoyer [23], Bureau of the Budget [7] and Willoughby [37], whereas Table 2 has been obtained from these three sources and from Fite and Reese [13], Primack and Willis [24] and Schnitzer [27]. These two tables lead to Table 3 which underlies the cycles in Chart 1.

Table 3
Data Underlying Chart 1

Decades	No. of New Regulatory Agencies Per Decade	No. of New Major Economic Laws Per Decade
1760-1770		4
1770-1780		16
1780-1790		8
1790-1800		7
1800-1810		10
1810-1820		7
1820-1830		6
1830-1840	1	9
1840-1850	0	5
1850-1860	0	5
1860-1870	2	18
1870-1880	1	10
1880-1890	1	10
1890-1900	1	14
1900-1910	1	14
1910-1920	14	57
1920-1930	3	31
1930-1940	11	48
1940-1950	24	80
1950-1960	4	41
1960-1970	12	73
1970-1980	20	125

Pattern and
Cause of Depressions

The ebb and flow that periodically occurs in GNP is commonly called the business cycle, which has characterized Western economies for as far back as we have the record. Economic activity usually passes through four phases—recession, depression, recovery and boom. When GNP and employment are declining the economy is said to be in a recession, which, when deep, becomes a depression. When output and employment are rising, the economy is said to be in a phase of recovery, which becomes a boom as full employment nears and industries operate at maximum capacity.

The present chapter is concerned mainly with an analysis of the declining phase of the business cycle. A recession usually lasts for one to three years during which the rate of unemployment, while rising, is generally below 12%. When a recession lasts for more than three years, and/or the rate of unemployment lies between 12% and 20%, then the economy may be said to be suffering from a depression. However, when business stagnates for six or more years, then the nation's plight may be called a great depression. Thus depending on its depth and length, the downswing of the business cycle may be called a recession, depression or a great depression.

All business contractions are bad, but depressions are disastrous and great depressions simply cataclysmic. As prosperous as U.S. economy has been since the Second World War, it too has passed through all types of convulsions in its long chronicle. It has frequently faced recessions, at times depressions, and, rarely, great depressions. This is a dilemma that has haunted Western society for a long time, and economists have periodically offered various cures for this ill. Yet, it is sad to note that the theory of business contraction is still seriously deficient. Despite the appearance of hundreds of hypotheses, all that economists have done is to provide a theory of recession, not of depression. However, before analyzing this issue, let us explore the historical record.

Pattern of Depressions

In the last three chapters we have seen that, except in the aftermath of the Civil War, inflation, regulation and money growth in U.S. economy have crested together every third decade over more than two centuries. These may be called regular or deterministic cycles because they uphold the controversial concept of historical determinism. Is there an identical cycle with respect to business activity or GNP? The answer is no. Yet a similar, though not exactly the same, pattern can be detected from the U.S. annals.

It turns out that in U.S. economy there have been at least one recession every decade, and a great depression every third or sixth decade in the sense that if the third decade managed to avoid a depression, then the next third decade experienced a cumulative effect—an all-time disaster. Thus the 1780s witnessed a depression, but the 1810s did not. Three decades later, the 1840s passed through an unprecedented crisis. The 1870s also suffered a great depression, but the 1900s did not. Hence thirty years later occurred the greatest depression in history. Let us see if this pattern accords with facts reported by others.

The Depression of 1780s

Data about business activity, as reported by the Cleveland Trust Company, goes as far back as 1790. For the 1780s, however, we have to rely on contemporary writings and books on history.

The course of the American economy in the 1770s was determined mainly by the revolution. Although there was a lot of destruction in some regions, many farmers and merchants prospered greatly from war. Those who were dependent on British markets were big losers as these markets were closed to their products. However, those who could sell their goods to British or American troops profited handsomely from hostilities. On the whole, though, the American economy flourished because of the war.

After the British defeat at Yorktown in October 1781, hostilities ceased for all practical purposes, and a downturn set in. Business activity began to decline in 1782, and after the peace treaty was signed in Paris in 1783, the economy slid into a depression, which was caused mainly by a huge deficit in the balance of trade. There was a great influx of British goods which were in heavy demand in the free nation. But they also depressed prices in American markets. However, foreign markets, because of protectionist policies of Britain and France, were not fully open to American goods. As a result, exports fell far short of imports, causing a massive deficit in U.S. balance of trade and a serious depression.

Although the economy began to move out of its slump in 1786, farm prices remained depressed well into 1787. Thus, from start to finish, the depression of the 1780s lasted five to six years, or from 1782-83 to 1787. Hence the 1780s experienced a serious, though perhaps not a great, depression.

The Great Depression of 1840s

The record of business cycles from 1790 to 1980 is illustrated in Charts 1 to 3, which deal with fluctuations in business activity around a long-term trend. If every year the economy grew at a constant rate, then its expansion path would be identical with a trend line which is also called the line of zero deviation. The vertical axis in the charts measures percentage oscillations, positive or negative, from the trend, whereas the horizontal axis represents time. Positive deviations reflect an economy in the upward phase of the cycle, whereas negative deviations represent economic contractions.

Part I of Chart 1 shows that between 1790 and 1820, there were many recessions but no depression, because no downturn lasted more than three years. Part II, however, reveals that the slump of 1840s endured for seven years from 1840 to 1846, because throughout this period business activity was below the trend line. This contraction, called the Debt Repudiation Depression, was clearly the worst until that time in U.S. history. Not only was it painfully long, it was also very deep, as the business activity, at one point, fell by more than 20%. Thus, the disaster of 1840s was clearly a great depression. Note that there was no depression in the 1810s, or at any other time between the 1790s and 1830s.

The Great Depression of 1870s

Part I of Chart 2 reveals a **seven-year-long** slump in the 1870s, which arrived three decades after the 1840s. This contraction began in 1873 and afflicted the economy until 1879. This was also a great depression.

Business Cycles Between 1790–1855

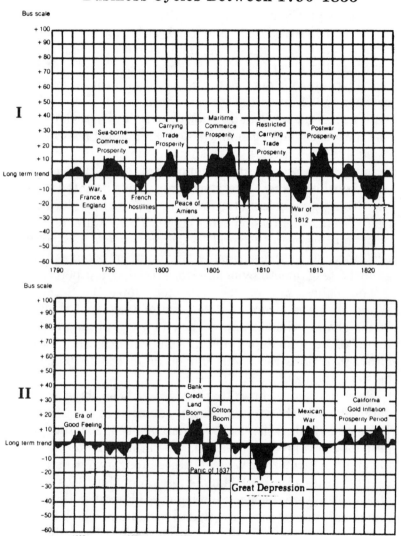

Source: Adapted from Cleveland Trust Co.

Chart 1

The Great Depression of 1930s

Part II of Chart 2 reveals that there was no great depression between 1890 and 1920, although two severe slumps occurred in the 1890s, the first between 1893 and 1895 and the other between 1896 and 1897.

Let us now consider Chart 3 which plots business cycles between 1920 and 1980, and shows that the 1930s experienced the worst depression of all time. This calamity was the longest—as economic activity remained below the trend line for ten years—as well as the deepest in history, because the economy at one point sank more than forty percent below the zero line. Here again it may be noted that the 1910s experienced no depression of any kind. Nor has there been a depression since 1940. There were minor recessions between 1945 and 1960; and between 1960 and 1980 there were severe slumps, but no depression, as the annual rate of unemployment never exceeded nine percent.

The highest rate of unemployment since the Second World War was recorded at the end of 1982, (not shown in the chart), when it approached 11%. In other words, there has been no depression in America since the 1930s, although serious recessions did occur in the 1970s and between 1980 and 1982.

Thus the record shows that there have been three great depressions in the United States, one each in the 1840s, 1870s and 1930s, whereas the slump of the 1780s, though perhaps not a great depression, was unprecedented as it lingered for five or six years. Of these four, two were the deepest in history. Both the depression of the 1840s and of the 1930s were the worst in memory. Thus, even though unlike inflation, money growth and regulation, which have jointly crested every third decade, depressions do not have an exact cycle, they have indeed followed a pattern, which in a way accords with the three-decade periodicity of the deterministic cycles.

The pattern of depressions, as noted before, is simply this. There has been at least one recession in every decade

Business Cycles Between 1855-1920

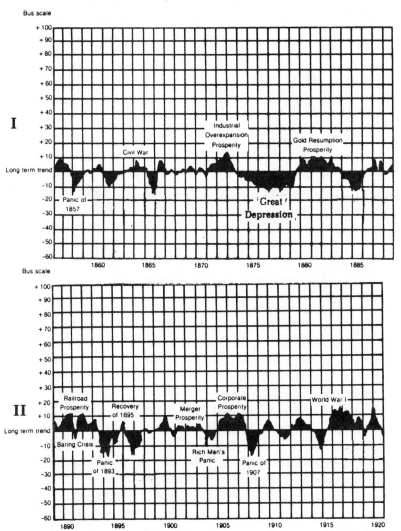

Source: Adapted from Cleveland Trust Co.

Chart 2

in the United States ever since its birth. But some recessions turned into great depressions, which arose every third or every sixth decade in the sense that if the third decade following the preceding crisis managed to avoid a great depression, then the next third decade suffered a cumulative effect—an economic blight worse than the previous worst. Thus the 1870s experienced a depression, but the 1810s did not, nor did any other decade until the 1840s, which witnessed a great depression that was the deepest until that time. Thirty years later, the 1870s, also passed through a great depression, but this was not as severe as the calamity of the 1840s. Another great depression was due in the 1900s, but none appeared at that time. Hence three decades later occured the greatest depression in history.

Conventional Wisdom on Depressions

What causes recessions and depressions? This question has haunted Western society for more than two centuries, eliciting a wide variety of theories and conjectures from economists. Yet all that the experts have produced so far is a general theory of recession rather than depression.

Conventional wisdom essentially revolves around the Keynesian mechanism determining a country's GNP, something we first analyzed in Chapter 3. Although the concepts introduced by Keynes have been greatly modified over the years, his basic premise remains intact. There is now a general agreement that the business cycle in American annals has been propelled mainly by fluctuations in aggregate demand for goods and services rather than by fluctuations in aggregate supply. Some downturns may indeed have been initiated by supply-side disturbances such as the sharp increase in oil prices in the 1970s, yet, by and large, recessions and depressions have been caused by contractions in aggregate demand.

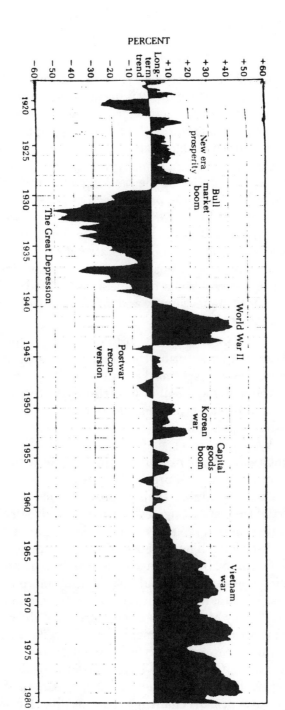

Business Cycles Between 1920–1980

Source: Adapted from the Ameri Trust Co.

Chart 3

121

Up to this point both Keynesians and Monetarists agree. Where they part company is in the question about the main source of fluctuations in aggregate demand which consists of total consumption, investment and government expenditure. Monetarists believe that money is the primary determinant of aggregate spending. When the Fed adds to the ability of the banking system to increase the supply of money, the private sector is able to borrow more funds than before at an acceptable rate of interest, and this in turn induces a rise in aggregate demand. This line of reasoning, then, establishes a strong connection between money supply and business activity. Monetarists believe that major recessions have been associated with absolute declines in money supply and minor ones with contractions in money growth.

In support of their view, Monetarists cite the experience of the economy during the great depression of the 1930s. There was a stock-market crash in October 1929 and it generated a good deal of uncertainty in the public, which reacted by way of increasing its withdrawal of cash from the banks. The Fed, which had been set up mainly to enable the system to meet such exigencies, failed to rescue the banks which were basically sound but were unable to meet the public's sudden proclivity for cash. Many banks failed as a result, ruining their depositors who were forced to curtail their spending, leading to successive declines in the business activity. Nearly 2000 banks suspended operations in 1931 alone. The collapse of the banking system, while the Fed stood by idly, caused a sharp drop in money supply, which, between 1929 and 1932, fell by more than a third.

Keynesians accept this scenario of the monetary collapse sketched by Monetarists. They agree that the Fed behavior in the 1930s was perverse. But they argue that instead of the falling money supply ushering a decrease in the GNP, the falling GNP could have caused a decline in money supply. This is a chicken and egg question: Which came first? Keynesians challenge the causality that Monetarists impute to money and GNP during the Great Depression. In support of their view, they cite the experience of Canadian and British economies in the 30s. The central bank in both Britain and Canada came to the rescue of the banking system and their bank failures were minor at that time. Yet their economies, especially that of Canada, were traumatized just as much as U.S. economy. Therefore the fall in money supply could not have been so crucial to the severity of the Great Depression.

To Keynesians, the depression of the 1930s was initiated in 1929 by a fall in investment and made worse by the inept fiscal policy of the government. As business activity fell, tax collections also declined. In order to balance its budget, the government raised its tax rates, and this, according to Keynesians, was a perverse policy, as the rise in taxes forced the public to further reduce its consumption, leading to a further fall in GNP and so on. Thus, the investment induced recession of 1929 turned into a depression because of the dubious fiscal policy of the government.

A synthetic view is that both monetary and fiscal policies were inept during the 1930s, and they turned what otherwise could have been a mild recession into the greatest depression ever. Thus conventional wisdom blames the catastrophe of the 30s on faulty policies of the government.

Inequality and Depressions

There are, however, a few facts that economists have slighted or ignored. True, monetary and fiscal policies were perverse around the Great Depression. But were they not perverse around every major recession of the 19th century? Friedman, the Patriarch of Monetarists, himself argues that money growth decreased around every recession in the United States in the 19th century. Similarly, Keynesians recognize that the government tended to balance its budget by raising taxes around every recession before the Second World War. The accepted doctrine in the pre-Keynesian days, after all, was that, as with a prudent household, government's expenses ought not exceed its income. Therefore if tax collection falls, as it usually does during a downturn, government should either trim its expenditure, raise taxes, or do both. Hence fiscal policy tended in the past to be restrictive whenever a recession occurred.

Clearly then both monetary and fiscal policies used to be erroneous around every recession, of which many had occurred before. There was nothing new about the remedies that were applied to the recession of 1929. Why then did it turn into the greatest economic calamity ever? What was its nemesis? In plain words, the issue is simply this: if faulty government policies did not create a major depression in the past, why did they create one in the 1930s?

There must have been some new factor at work in 1929. There must have been some other parameter which has eluded the experts so far.

There is a large body of economic literature emphasizing the fact that recessions are caused by the unequal distribution of income. Keynes himself pointed this out as one reason for the rise in savings and hence for the inadequacy of aggregate demand. Since the rich have a higher propensity to save than the poor, concentration of income in a few hands induces an increase in aggregate savings.

Now savings did increase as income inequality rose during the 1920s. Many sections of society had then failed to share in the national prosperity. However, economists recognize that this rise in savings was not sharp enough to generate a crisis of the magnitude of the Great Crash. It was perhaps sufficient to initiate a recession but not a cataclysm severe enough to engulf the whole world.

The wave of business mergers that occurred during the 1920s is sometimes cited as another cause of the Great Depression. Many monopolies, oligopolies, and other industrial colossi had then emerged almost overnight to induce a highly inefficient economy. This led to a fall in investment and hence in aggregate demand. But here again the fall was not large enough to generate a world-wide crisis that was the worst in history. Indeed, such industrial concentration had occurred before, especially during the 1880s and late 1890s, but had produced no similar disaster.

What, then, was the real cause of the Great Depression? What is the parameter that has so far escaped the scholars?

My contention is that this new parameter was the concentration of wealth, which peaked in 1929 and gave rise to the Great Depression. During the 1920s, there was a sudden and sharp surge in the disparity of wealth. Table 1 shows that in 1922 barely one percent of U.S. families owned 31.6% of national wealth, but by 1929, within seven years, their share had risen to 36.3%. This is a rather sharp jump in wealth concentration, which, barring some unprecedented disturbances or misguided policies, usually takes a long time to change. For instance, between 1933 and 1969, the share of top wealth-holders varied between 28.3% and 24.9%—a fairly small variation. Their share, of course, dropped drastically between 1929 and 1933. This was a direct result of the Great Depression which wiped out many fortunes. In addition to the sharp rise in inequality during the 1920s, the share of the top wealth-holders in 1929 was the highest in history.

What is the connection between the inequity of wealth and a depression? To understand this, it is necessary to reexamine the difference between a recession and a depression. A recession occurs when GNP begins to fall or its growth fails to keep pace with the growth in labor force, so that the rate of unemployment begins to rise. A depression occurs when a recession is accompanied by a collapse of the financial system. Many businesses then vanish, the public loses confidence in its banks, and unemployment climbs to levels unprecedented in recent memory. U.S. history reveals that in a recession, unemployment is no higher than 12%, whereas in a depression it may go as high as 25%. As noted before, there have been numerous recessions in the United States but only three great depressions, and each time it was the massive public flight from banks that turned an ordinary fall in GNP into a disaster.

What causes a financial panic? To understand this, let us examine the behavior of a typical bank, which, we assume, is interested in making loans at the highest possible interest rate so that its profits are maximized. Normally the bank lends money to a credit-worthy individual or business, which is unlikely to default on the loan. But at times the bank may make risky loans with a high potential for failure. This happens especially when competition among banks is high in securing borrowers deposits.

When wealth becomes concentrated, three effects normally occur. First, the number of persons with few or no assets rises. As a result the demand for loans increases, because the borrowing needs of the poor or the middle income groups far exceed those of the affluent. Second, since the poor and the middle-class people, who are in a majority, now have fewer assets, the borrowers in general become less credit-worthy than before. If a bank rejects risky borrowers, its financial structure remains sound. But in an environment where credit-worthiness has generally deteriorated, most banks cannot afford to be choosy, especially when they have to pay interest on their deposits. Only a prudent bank then avoids making risky loans.

The upshot of this discussion is that as the concentration of wealth rises, the number of banks with relatively shaky loans also rises. And the higher is this concentration, the greater is the number of potential bank failures.

A side-effect of the growing wealth disparity is the rise in speculative investments. It is a well known fact that, as a person becomes wealthy, his aversion to risk declines. This is the celebrated Arrow-Pratt hypothesis of decreasing absolute risk aversion. As the wealth inequity grows, the overall riskiness of investments made by the rich also grows, giving rise to a speculative fever in the end. It essentially reflects the human urge to make a quick profit. It means margin or installment buying of assets and goods only for resale and not for productive purposes. It means, for instance, increasing involvement of investors in futures

Table 1

Share of Wealth Held by the Richest 1 Percent

Year	Share of Wealth Held by 1 Percent of U.S. Adults or Families
1810	21.0
1860	24.0
1870	27.0
1900	26.0- 31.0
1922	31.6
1929	36.3
1933	28.3
1939	30.6
1945	23.3
1949	20.8
1953	27.5
1956	26.0
1958	26.9
1962	27.4
1965	29.2
1969	24.9

Sources: This table, minus the 1870 figure, appears in Turner and Starnes [32, p. 19], who cite Gallman [16], and Smith and Franklin [28] as their sources. The 1870 figure is obtained from Soltow [29, p. 103].

markets. As firms or individuals see others profiting quickly from speculative purchases, they tend to follow suit. As Kindleberger aptly puts it:

> When the number of firms and households indulging in these practices grows large, bringing in segments of population that are normally aloof from such ventures, speculation for profit leads away from such normal, rational behavior to what have been described as "manias" or "bubbles." The word "mania" emphasizes the irrationality; "bubble" foreshadows the bursting.
> . . . The object of speculation may vary widely from one mania or bubble to the next. It may involve primary products, or goods manufactured for export to distant markets, domestic and foreign securities of various kinds, contracts to buy or sell goods or securities, land in the country or city, houses, office buildings, shopping centers, condominiums, foreign exchange. At a late stage, speculation tends to detach itself from really valuable objects and turn to delusive ones. A larger and larger group of people seeks to become rich without a real understanding of the process involved. Not surprisingly swindlers and catchpenny schemes flourish [19, p. 19].

As Kindleberger points out, speculative fever tends to feed on itself, and the general population seeks to join it at a late stage. This is the same as Minsky's financial instability hypothesis. But the speculative fever cannot begin in the absence of wealth disparity, for only the very rich as a class are willing and can afford to squander money on assets with a high but relatively illusive return. In other words, wealth inequity is a prerequisite for manias and bubbles. The greater is the inequity, the bigger is the bubble, and the more painful is its eventual bursting.

In short, the concentration of wealth has two pernicious effects on the economy, as it increases the number of banks with shaky loans, and fuels the speculative frenzy in which eventually even the banking system is caught.

As long as the economy is healthy, borrowers are in a position to pay back the loans and the financial system goes on functioning smoothly. However, as soon as aggregate demand falls for any reason, some goods go unsold, business inventories rise, output falls and some workers are laid off. A few businesses and banks also then fail. This, of course, typically occurs during a recession. Soon inventories are depleted as output declines faster than demand, and producers regain confidence to raise production and recall fired workers, with the economy resuming its path of expansion.

The depth of the recession depends on the extent of prevailing wealth disparity that raises the number of fragile banks and nourishes speculative bubbles, which always burst in the end. Whenever a bank fails, there occurs some fall in total deposits and money supply and hence a further fall in aggregate demand and output. Therefore, higher concentration of wealth, by increasing the number of fragile banks, produces a deeper recession.

Under capitalism wealth disparity tends to rise in the long run. A time comes when this disparity, and the concomitant number of shaky banks, become so high that any recession can then cause a collapse of the financial system. The bursting of the speculative bubble, another direct consequence of inequity, only adds fuel to the fire. Money supply, aggregate demand, output and employment then move in a downward spiral, and an ordinary recession turns into a depression. And if the speculative bubble is extremely large, then its bursting gives rise to a great depression. In the aftermath, the concentration of wealth also declines, because many fortunes are then wiped out.

The inequity in wealth ownership does not develop overnight: It derives mainly from inheritance. Usually it takes at least a generation before wealth is transferred to posterity and its distribution becomes critically unequal. That is why we find that in U.S. history while recessions have frequently occurred, depressions have been rare, usually spread by one or two generations.

Table 1 shows that the wealth disparity in 1929 was the steepest ever, and it is well known that the speculative loans made by the banks were also at their zenith at that time. No wonder then, an ordinary recession of 1929 turned into an unprecedented economic disaster. (McElvaine [22, pp. 37-50] gives other reasons why wealth disparity caused the Great Depression).

Since the 1930s, wealth disparity has been on the decline. That is why the economy has succeeded in avoiding depressions of any kind, even though it has had a close brush with severe recessions, as during 1973-75 and 1980-82.

Table 1 shows that the disparity of wealth was also high in 1870, when, as the record reveals, there occurred a wave of speculation in railroad securities and in the New York stock market, which eventually crashed in September 1873 leading to the great depression of the 1870s.

For the 1840s we lack any precise figure on the disparity of wealth. However Williamson and Lindert conclude that "the wealth concentration rose over most of the period 1774-1860, with especially steep increases from the 1830s to the late 1840s." [36, p. 46]. Whatever evidence there is points to the fact that there was a sharp jump in wealth inequity during the 1830s, which experienced a speculative frenzy in land and cotton, culminating in the crisis of 1839 and the great depression of the 1840s.

The upshot of our discussion so far is that conventional wisdom only provides a theory of recession, which is caused by a decline in aggregate demand. It lacks an adequate explanation for the surge of speculative manias which have always preceded an economic crisis. It also fails to explain the fragility of the banking system, which collapses to generate a financial panic. Both these effects spring from high wealth disparities. Hence the real cause of great depressions in the past, or of depressions of any kind, was not faulty government policies but extreme inequity in the distribution of wealth. A depression, in a nutshell, is the result of a financial panic, accompanying a recession.

Perverse Fiscal Policy of the 1920s

Keynesians contend that the fiscal policy of the early 1930s was perverse as the government attempted to balance its budget by raising taxes, whereas it should have done just the opposite to stimulate aggregate demand. There is no doubt that this type of fiscal action worsened the situation, but without a fragile financial system it could not have caused the catastrophe.

Seeds of the Great Depression were actually sown by the truly perverse fiscal policies in the 1920s, when the government reduced taxes in 1921, 1924, 1926 and 1928. These tax cuts were very favorable to big business and high-income groups. The concentration of wealth was already high in the early 1920s, when, as Table 1 reveals, barely one percent of U.S. families owned almost a third of national wealth. Reducing taxes of the opulent was then a truly perverse policy. There is nothing wrong with cutting taxes and the size of the government. Big government adds to economic inefficiency and mismanagement. But easing the tax burden of the multimillionaires—that is something else. Nothing but increasing wealth disparity and hence eventual calamity come from it.

The result was inevitable. Tax cuts of the 1920s generated the sharpest rise in wealth concentration in just a matter of seven years. Between 1922 and 1929, the rich became richer as never before. Consequently, the attendant banking system was the shakiest and the speculative bubble the largest in history. So was the eventual collapse of the economy.

Thus, while the fiscal policy of the early 1930s was somewhat perverse, the truly perverse tax policy had occurred in the 1920s, when the reduced tax burden of the affluent planted the germ of the Great Crash.

7

The Great Depression
of 1990-96

It is time to weave various strands together and see what
we have learned from history, which, as is clear by now, has
its own rhythm. We have discovered that inflation, money
growth and regulation have all followed a clear-cut and
deterministic path, and while the behavior of great
depressions is not so apparent, they, too, have had a
definite pattern. While the cycles of inflation, money
growth and regulation have all crested together every third
decade for over two centuries, great depressions have
occurred at intervals of three or six decades.

A burning question of the day is: Can it happen again?
Is another great depression possible? This thought, which
comes up every time the economy is in distress, has
haunted the public since the early 1970s, when a sharp
surge in the price of oil generated the most serious
recession since the Second World War. It is an issue that
has revived interest in the theory of the business cycle,
which many in the 1960s regarded as obsolete and dead;
however, the cycle is well and alive. It has recently inspired
a spate of books by notable thinkers such as Temin [30],
Brunner [6], Kindleberger [19], Volcker [35], Saint-
Etienne [25] among others.

Much of the new energy is directed at understanding
what really caused the depression of the 1930s. Few

directly address themselves to the question: is a new great depression possible? My answer is that not only is another 1930s-style tragedy possible, it is, given the perverse fiscal policy of the Reagan Presidency, inevitable. But before I expound on my conclusion, let us see what others have to say about this question.

Dornbusch and Fischer, authors of one of the best-selling texts on macroeconomics, speak of the possible recurrence of the Great Depression in this way:

> On the question of whether it could happen again, there is agreement that it could not, except, of course, in the event of truly perverse policies. But these are less likely now than they were then. For one thing we have history to help us avoid its repetition. Taxes would not again be raised in the middle of a depression nor would attempts be made to balance the budget. The Fed would seek actively to keep the money supply from falling. In addition, the government now has a much larger role in the economy than it did then. The high level of government spending, which is relatively slow to change, and automatic stabilizers, including the income tax, unemployment insurance, and Social Security, give the economy more stability than it had then. [11, p. 547].

In a front page article entitled "Economists Don't See Threats to Economy Portending Depression," *The Wall Street Journal* (October 12, 1984) echoes the same sentiment. There Clark and Malabre, reflecting the majority view of scholars, conclude that

> . . . the public should have—if anything —more confidence than before that an economic crackup like that in the 1930s won't happen

again. That at least is the judgment of 10 eminent analysts.

The article reflects the opinion of established economists including three Nobel Laureates and two former chiefs of the Federal Reserve Board. According to the *Journal*, this group has consistently maintained that another 1930s-style calamity is not likely. Paul Samuelson, a Nobel Laureate, is quoted as saying, "Another depression on the order of the 1930s just doesn't seem possible." The attitude of Arthur Burns, the Fed chairman under Presidents Nixon, Ford and Carter, is much the same. The *Journal* reports him as saying, "I still see no new Great Depression in the cards for the simple reason that the government can prevent collapse, and the government will prevent it." In addition to these eminent scholars, the *Journal* cites Geoffrey Moore, John Galbraith, William Martin, Milton Friedman, Lawrence Klein, Martin Feldstein, Robert Hall and Charles Kindleberger as those convinced that another great depression is not in prospect.

These economists are among the best that the profession has to offer. Some of them are indeed concerned about government actions. Galbraith is worried about the resurgence of inflation, while Martin fears the detrimental effects of financial deregulation. Friedman is apprehensive about the consequences of international debt, whereas Feldstein is concerned about unprecedented budget deficits. Many of them are anxious about growing popularity of protectionism.

They are all, however, quite optimistic about the future course of the American economy. While they may disagree over the true cause of the Great Depression, they are all convinced that such an event is unlikely to recur—at least not in the near future. Usual reasons cited for this optimism are that the government will not repeat the policy mistakes of the 1930s. Taxes will not again be raised in the midst of a recession, nor will money supply be allowed to fall so sharply.

The scholars cited by the *Wall Street Journal* undoubtedly carry considerable weight. They have made impressive contributions to economics. But I submit that if they had seen my evidence, they perhaps would agree with me. Testimony of the long-run cycles presented in earlier chapters points to only one direction, namely, that another economic disaster, possibly worse than the previous catastrophe, is now in the making. The cycles of money, inflation and regulation, and the pattern of great depressions are remarkable for their longevity and antiquity. They have endured phenomenal changes in American economy and society, except, of course, the carnage casused by the Civil War. They have survived the onslaught of industrial revolutions, breath-taking inventions, two world wars, waves of regulation and business mergers, creation of the Fed, the New Deal, the Atomic Age, the voyage to the moon, the Computer, the Watergate, the Gold Standard, the Dollar Standard and myriad social movements. And that which has lived so long amid numerous convulsions is bound to persist in the future as well. Barring another Civil War, the stranglehold of these cycles can be broken only by fundamental economic reforms, which are discussed in Chapter 9.

Relationship Among Cycles

Let us see what the essential message of the long-run cycles, including the law of social cycle is. Chapter 2 argues that ever since the 1860s the West has been in its second age of acquisitors. Now this age was at its zenith in the 1920s. That is why the Great Depression only produced economic calamity but not a political change, as the affluent have continued to dominate society. But since the 1930s, the influence of acquisitors has been on the decline in the sense that not the rich themselves but their hired intellectuals have been running the levers of government.

Hence if a depression occurs in the current milieu, not only will the economy collapse, the political structure will also be transformed.

Every age passes through two phases—the rising phase and the declining phase. During the ascending period, the dominant class is clearly on top and its reign is more or less unchallenged. During the descending period, however, troubles begin to mount and the ruler turns to intellectuals for advice. Hence during the declining phase the upper class continues to rule but only with the help of advisers belonging to the class of intellectuals. And during the downswing of the acquisitive era, the intellectuals also turn into acquisitors.

Since the 1930s there has been a rise in the pro-interventionist sentiment, which signifies that it is the government's responsibility to cure all social ills. But in order to translate this idea into reality, intellectuals are needed first to devise and then to enforce regulations. That is why it is the intellectual acquisitor, rather than the "pure" acquisitor, who has been dominant in Western society since the 1930s. This is the surest sign that the age of acquisitors has been in the downswing ever since, and may be ready to breathe its last. (For a further analysis of this point, see Batra [1, ch. 9]).

With the age of acquisitors on the down hill, a major economic crisis today will cause a political upheaval in the West. During the 1920s, the era of the wealthy was at its zenith; therefore all that the Great Crash did was to transfer power from "pure" acquisitors to intellectual acquisitors. But there was no change in the ruling class itself, as super materialsim, the basic ideology of acquisitors, continued to permeate the social psyche. However, if a catastrophe hits the economy in the future, a new class will come to power.

Chapters 3 and 4 show that U.S. economy, except in the aftermath of the Civil War, has, over the past two centuries, experienced long-run cycles of inflation and money growth, jointly peaking every third decade. Since such a peak last appeared in the 1970s, then, barring another cataclysm resembling the Civil War, the 1990s will experience sharply low money growth and further disinflation, if not outright deflation.

Chapter 5 displays that U.S. economy has also experienced a long-run decennial cycle of regulation which jointly crests with the other two cycles. Moreover, at least during the 20th century, the peak years of regulation have been followed by a decade of deregulation, and then by another surge in regulation reflected in socio-economic reforms, culminating in high inflation. Thus the regulatory cycle crested in the 1910s, troughed in the 1920s, but started rising again in the 1930s. Similarly, it crested in the 1940s, troughed in the 1950s and resumed its climb in the 1960s. In the 1970s, it peaked again. The 1980s, not surprisingly, are experiencing deregulation; similarly, the 1990s will be a decade of socio-economic reforms leading to another rise in regulation.

During the 1930s economic institutions were reformed under the New Deal; during the 1960s social and economic institutions underwent reforms stimulated by the Civil Rights Movement. Since the regulatory cycle, under the influence of intellectual acquisitors, reveals an upward trend, reforms of the 1990s will not just be social and economic, they will also be political in character. This means that society will then be traumatized in more spheres than in the decades of 1930s and 1960s. It may be noted that this inference accords well with the conclusion about the political transformation mentioned above. The cycle of regulation, therefore, is in harmony with the all-encompassing law of social cycle.

Chapter 6 argues that wealth disparity gives rise to a shaky banking system and to a speculative bubble, which bursts when a recession hits. The combination of a recession and the collapse of the banking system generates a depression. In 1929, the inequity of wealth was at its zenith, as just 1% of U.S. families owned over 36% of national wealth. Consequently, the 1930s experienced an all-time economic disaster, accompanied by the sharpest deflation ever.

The Depression of 1990s

Chapter 6 also demonstrated that, as with money, inflation and regulation, great depressions, too, have followed a certain pattern in the United States. Every third or sixth decade was a decade of great depression in the sense that if the third decade managed to avoid a crisis, then the subsequent third decade experienced a cumulative decline—an all-time disaster. Thus the 1780s witnessed a serious depression, but the 1810s did not. Hence, the 1840s underwent the worst depression of the times. The 1870s also suffered a great depression, but the 1900s did not. Hence the 1930s went through a carnage worse than the previous worst.

The message of cycles must now be crystal clear. Since the 1960s escaped a great depression, the 1990s will experience another cumulative effect—the worst economic crisis in history.

The germ of this calamity has already been planted by the misguided fiscal policy of the Reagan administration. During the 1920s, the pro-business, pro-affluent tax cuts caused a sharply higher concentration of wealth, which eventually led to the collapse of the economy. During the 1980s, the pro-wealthy tax cuts are producing the same effects. The inequity of wealth is now climbing at an unprecedented pace. Within a few years, this inequity will surpass even its peak reached in 1929. This is because currently there are two factors operating to raise the disparity. Low or zero taxes paid by the affluent is only one cause. The historically high rate of interest, itself the product of wealth concentration, is another.

When the return on investment rises, the opulent are the main beneficiaries. Soon the wealth disparity will reach an all-time high, exceeding even the pinnacle of 1929. Signs of this disparity are now everywhere, but its dangers, for lack of proper understanding, are not being recognized. A recession is due in 1989-90, and this, combined with a shaky banking system created by the unprecented concentration of wealth, will give rise to the unprecedented depression of the 1990s.

The 1920s and the 1980s

We can actually pinpoint 1990 as the year of the world's greatest depression ever. The analysis of previous chapters has demonstrated that U.S. economy undergoes major cycles every third decade. Since our data is aggregated over a decade, this means that every 28 to 32 years a significant transformation occurs in the American economy and society. However, a deeper study of the 20th century data reveals that cyclical similarities in the economy are more striking over the sixty year intervals—twice the length of the three-decade cycle. In this connection let us compare the 1920s with major economic events occurring between 1980 and 1984, the year of the present writing.

First, let us examine general trends; later we will make a year-by-year comparison. We have already seen that the 1920s were marked by low money growth, low inflation, and deregulation. In these respects the 1980s have so far resembled the 1920s. The same holds true with the merger activity among businesses. Both decades reveal a sharp rise in industrial marriages and concentration.

The most profitable sector during the 1920s was the automobile industry, which also earned record profits in 1983 and 1984, with prospects of further increases in 1985 and 1986. Reasons for such high earnings, of course, differ between the two decades, but the outcome is nonetheless the same. In general, high-technology industries experienced a sharp growth in the 20s. The same is true so far in the 80s.

Banks earned mediocre incomes during the 20s. They have done much the same in the first half of the 80s. Then, as now, the farm-sector was highly depressed because of the loss of foreign markets and the low prices received by American farmers. Then, as now, the coal industry was in the doldrums. So were textiles, shoes, shipping and the railroads, as they are now. Energy prices declined throughout the 20s. They have done the same so far in the 80s.

The 1920s were the decade of a Republican Presidency with a strikingly pro-business and anti-labor attitude. The 1980s are exactly alike in this respect. Then, as now, monetary policy of the Fed reflected Monetarist views. Then, as now, eminent economists were convinced that a prolonged depression was impossible, although their logic was totally different. Experts then believed that the capitalist system has an automatic mechanism that tends to cure all its ills including the problem of unemployment: No help is needed from the government. Today few have faith in that automatic mechanism; rather, the majority opinion among scholars now is that the government knows enough to prevent another crisis. Despite major ideological differences among them, experts are confident that no new great depression is in prospect, just as they were during the 1920s. In fact, two prominent economists of the day, Irving Fisher and Dennis Robertson, gave solemn assurances to the world on the very eve of the economic catastrophe.

There are, of course, some major differences between the decades in question. The government budget showed a surplus during the 20s, whereas it has shown huge deficits so far in the 80s and is likely to do so in the foreseeable future. Rates of interest were low at that time; they have been at record high during the 80s. The U.S. then enjoyed a big surplus in its balance of trade. It has been suffering unprecedented arrears for the last four years.

These striking disparities between the two decades simply reveal that the West's age of acquisitors, at zenith during the 1920s, is now gasping for breath. Actually one should not be surprised at the differences, for they are only to be expected over time. The surprising part is in all the similarities that we have detected. And that is where the regular cycles come in.

Let us now turn to the year-to-year comparison. The year 1920 experienced a recession, and so did 1980. As a result, the incumbent President, Woodrow Wilson, who was a Democrat, lost to a Republican named Warren Harding. In 1980 also the incumbent President, James Carter, belonging to the Democratic Party, was defeated by a Republican named Ronald Reagan. As Presidents, both Wilson and Carter were unable to persuade Congress to ratify legislation in the area of foreign policy. Congress refused to go along with Wilson and let the U.S. join the League of Nations. Similarly, Carter failed to persuade legislators to ratify the arms-limitations agreement between the U.S. and Russia.

The auto-sector is very important to the economy and General Motors (GM) is the dominant firm in this industry. It is a well-known saying that what is good for GM is good for America. In 1920 the auto giant had its first loss. The next time it lost money was in 1980. This is simply astounding, because the company earned profits even during calamitous years of the Great Depression. But as soon as 60 years passed, it incurred a loss. In 1920 many interest rates surged to their highest levels. The same thing happened in 1980. Both years, of course, were highly inflationary.

The major economic news of 1981 was a tax cut regarded as the biggest in history. The last time the "biggest" tax cut occurred was in the 1920s, starting with 1921. That year the President made a big name by crushing a strike of federal employees, the policemen. In 1981 also the

President won fame by crushing the strike of federal employees—the air traffic controllers.

In 1921 there was a sharp rise in unemployment. Similarly in 1981. Moreover, in both years the rise in unemployment was created by the tight money policies of the Fed.

The highlight of 1982 was a steep decline in interest rates along with a sharp rise in the stock market. The same occurred in 1922. In addition inflation came down in both years.

The major economic change of 1983 was that banks began to offer interest on checking accounts. The last time this occurred was in 1923, although towards its end. But in the 1930s banks were deprived of their authority, and Congress had to repeal its old legislation. Similarly, the stock market continued to rise in both years. In addition, both years experienced very sharp declines in unemployment.

In 1924 inflation remained low and unemployment continued to decline, while interest rates remained stable. The story of 1984 was much the same. Furthermore, in both years the Democratic candidate was defeated in the presidential election, leaving the Republican Party in power.

Thus we see that many events occurring between 1980 and 1984 are strikingly similar to those occurring between 1920 and 1924. Clearly, while the three-decade cycle exists, the six-decade cycle is more pronounced. In other words, every sixty odd years many major economic events in America tend to repeat themselves.

Taking the comparison to its logical end, 1985 will be a year of slow-down as was 1925 at its beginning. But in 1926 the economy expanded briskly, came to a standstill in 1927 and resumed its growth in 1928, lasting till the middle of 1929. Accordingly, we should expect the economy to prosper in 1986, lose a little steam in 1987 and then remain strong until 1989. All this time, inflation will be stable at the current rate of approximately 4.5% per year, and interest rates, while still historically high, will be more or less unchanged until 1988 and then rise significantly in 1989. Energy and farm prices will keep declining relative to other prices, although the oil price could rise in 1986.

The stock market will continue to rise, though not at the brisk pace of the 1920s. This is because the record high budget deficit of the 1980s is a depressant that did not exist at that time. Regardless of the stock market behavior, the speculative activity will increase sharply in the rest of the 1980s. So will the merger activity among industries.

At the end of 1989 or in the first half of 1990, the stock market will crash and will be followed by an abysmal decline in business activity and a sharply high rate of unemployment. The low point of this great depression will come in 1994. All in all the crisis will last at least seven years, from 1990 to 1996.

International Aspects

The depression of the 1930s was a world-wide event. America, Europe and the Third World were all, one way or another, caught in its throes. However, in some European countries, the crisis had actually begun as early as 1926, although the collapse did not come until after 1929.

While U.S. economy remained prosperous during much of the 1920s, the British economy was anemic. Britain suffered from severe unemployment throughout the decade, especially after the General Strike of 1926. Many industries such as coal, steel, shipbuilding, textiles and housing were depressed. The rate of unemployment, which was concentrated in Wales and the Northeast, rose to 9.6% in 1921, and slowly declined thereafter.

In 1926 Britain experienced a severe recession and its GNP declined by more than 4%, with unemployment soaring again. The economy recovered somewhat by 1929, but unemployment remained high.

The situation in France was much the same. Between 1924 and 1927 the French GNP was stagnant and unemployment reached a new high. In addition, the Franc plummeted because of high government debt. Between 1980 and 1984, the French unemployment has hovered around 9% and the Franc has been under constant pressure, falling to its lowest level in 1984. The British recession of 1926 also spread its tentacles to the French economy, which eventually recovered fast enough to share the prosperity of the American boom of 1928-29.

The situation in Germany was much worse than in Britain and France. The German economy suffered from hyper-inflation caused by enormous growth of money by the government. Between 1922 and 1923, inflation was simply devastating. The government introduced a new currency in 1923 and also pared its deficit. An international loan in 1924 resulted in much needed economic stability. But in 1926, unemployment surged to 8%. It was not until 1927 that the German economy recovered from combinations of inflationary psychology, the resulting financial collapse, and recession.

While Western Europe was in economic doldrums in the early 1920s, Central Europe fared no better. The Hapsburg Empire was dissolved after the First World War, but the countries that rose on its debris were too weak to have a viable economy. Both Austria and Hungary were in serious financial trouble right from their birth. It is only after their finances were put under international scrutiny that some degree of stability was achieved. After 1927, however, their economies, fueled by capital inflows from abroad, boomed.

The crux of this whole discussion is that 1926 was a year of serious economic problems in Europe, while the American economy, by and large, managed to avoid the slump. In view of the sixty-year cycle, 1986-87 will be the years of a severe recession in Europe, while the U.S. will continue to blossom.

Throughout the 1980s, as with the 1920s, Western Europe has suffered from high unemployment. At the time of this writing, unemployment in Britain is 13% and close to 10% in France, Germany and Belgium. The recession of 1986 will create depression-like conditions in some countries, especially Britain, France and Germany where unemployment will surge again. Between 1987 and 1989 Europe will recover somewhat, but its problem of unemployment will remain. When depression afflicts America in 1990, Europe, too, will suffer in the same proportion and so will the rest of the world.

Canada is one country whose economy is totally linked with that of the United States. Between 1982-84 unemployment in Canada has averaged around 11%. But, as with the U.S., the Canadian unemployment will steadily decline until 1989. After 1990, however, it will soar to the highest level ever.

International economic ills of the 1980s are reminiscent of those of the 1920s, but their dimensions have grown drastically. The main threat to the world economy today springs from the huge international debt of the Third World and the rising chorus of protectionism in America. The debt problem resembles the problem of war reparations facing Germany and its trading partners, especially France, during the 1920s. However, the international-debt load today is much heavier and afflicts many more countries than in the past. The war-reparations problem pales before the current affliction of the world debt.

Another major threat to international stability stems from growing protectionist demands in the U.S. The same had occurred during the 1920s, but at that time the foreign-trade sector was small relative to the rest of the American economy. By now the share of exports in U.S. GNP has more than doubled, and if the government gives in to protectionist pressures, the potential for damage is much higher today than ever before.

Protectionism means reducing foreign access to domestic markets. When one country creates such barriers, others usually follow suit, so that there is a general contraction in international trade, resulting in diminished business activity everywhere. The world is much more interdependent today than in the past. Hence, protectionist pressures should be resisted at all cost. If not, the world-wide depression will be much deeper than otherwise.

The diminution of world trade, however, may be unavoidable. Trade requires credit, which, because of colossal foreign debts, is growing scarce. A time might come when banks refuse all lending to debtor countries. That will then precipitate a crisis and eventually a world-wide depression.

Strategy for Investment

The previous chapter argues that, given the perverse fiscal policy of the Reagan Presidency, the depression of 1990 is now inevitable. The supporting evidence for this conclusion comes from a wide spectrum of sources including the long-run patterns of money, inflation, regulation and depressions, and above all the law of social cycle.

What can a person do now to prepare for this eventuality? 1990 is still five years away. There is still time before we are hit by the calamity.

There is a story in the *Old Testament* in which Joseph, a nobody, interprets the Pharaoh's dream, saying that there will be seven years of plenty followed by seven years of famine. He goes on to advise the king to store food and grain from his surplus and take other steps in preparation for the impending catastrophe.

This Biblical parable applies equally to our times. All evidence shows that there will be seven years of prosperity between 1983 and 1989, followed by seven years of economic drought between 1990 and 1996. We have to prepare for this disaster now, while there is time.

It is worth pointing at the outset that all preparatory steps should be aimed at surviving the impending crisis rather than profiting from it. This is because the crisis itself will be the result of relentless greed, of human propensity to make a quick buck, of unbounded faith in materialsim.

Therefore any strategy designed to benefit from the coming depression is bound to be ruinous in the end.

During a depression unemployment rises drastically and earnings of the employed sharply fall. But until 1989 the economy will be fairly prosperous. Therefore one should increase one's savings at this time, avoiding frivolous and unnecessary purchases. Spending on luxury items should be greatly reduced, if not eliminated. This may be an austere regimen, but it will pay off later. Even if someone thinks that my conclusions are wrong and another depression is impossible, the strategy of saving money cannot hurt. One can always buy things later.

How much money should one save between now and 1990? Assuming the worst-case scenario where a person loses his job and has to live totally on his assets, a family of four would need about $7,500 per year to survive the depression. At today's prices, the official poverty line begins at an annual income approximating $10,000. If prices were to decline 25% during the depression, then $7,500 would be able to buy subsistence. If one remains unemployed for, say, four years, a saving of about $30,000 will be sufficient for an average family to live through the worst of the crisis.

The next question is: how should savings be invested? My prognosis is that the remaining years of the 1980s will experience stable rates of inflation, interest and unemployment, with the stock market slowly rising up to 1989. This means that all assets, which profit from inflation, should be avoided. Real estate, for instance, will not make a good investment; nor will paintings, jewelry, or diamonds.

Stocks and bonds, in a non-inflationary environment, are preferable to real estate, but they ought to be non-speculative. In general one should avoid inordinately risky assets, which yield high return but can also lead to heavy losses.

Gold is not a good investment in disinflationary times, but its value usually rises during a crisis, where people lose confidence in paper currencies. But gold yields no return, while stocks, bonds and certificates of deposit do. Since the economy will be relatively stable until 1989, the purchase of gold as a safe-haven is not advisable until then, unless its price comes down from the current $300 range to the range of $200 per ounce.

Gold coins are preferable to bullion. The Canadian Maple-Leaf coin is the best in this connection, because it is also a legal tender in Canada, that is, it serves as currency as well.

By the end of 1988 or the middle of 1989, one should sell all one's holdings of stocks and real estate. Bonds may be kept but only of extremely safe and reliable companies with low short and long-term debt. Firms which survived the crisis of the 1930s will likely survive another in the future.

Prices fall dramatically during a depression. Hence all stocks and real estate then lose value. The price of gold, however, may not decline much, or may even rise, provided the public confidence in the currency is badly shaken. The depression of the 1990s is likely to be the worst in history. Therefore, some holding of gold after 1989 is advisable.

Another major casualty of a depression is the financial system. Many banks then collapse and their depositors are ruined. In spite of the federal insurance currently available to deposits, hundreds of banks will fail in the 1990s, resulting in heavy losses to some people. Cash will be much safer than bank accounts at that time.

In short, the investment strategy during the 1980s and 1990s has to be cautious and prudent. One should do the following:

1.   Spend less, save more now;

2.   Invest in nonspeculative stocks and bonds;

3. Avoid real estate and, until 1989, gold, unless its price falls close to $200 per ounce;

4. Sell all stocks and real estate in 1989, but keep the bonds of extremely sound companies, especially those that lived through the depression of the 1930s;

5. After 1989, save in the form of cash, gold and safe bonds.*

*This book is designed to give an advance warning to the public about the coming depression. It is not about a get-rich scheme. Instead, it furnishes a defensive and conservative strategy to survive the impending economic disaster. Its purpose is to educate the public and offer general but not specific guidance. The author, Venus Books and anyone else associated with this work are not responsible to any individual or entity for any profit or loss alleged to be caused by the investment advice or information contained in this book. Circumstances differ from person to person. If anyone wants specific advice, then he/she should contact the author directly.

9

How Can We Prevent
Another Depression?

Napoleon was fond of saying that the word "impossible"
exists in the dictionary of fools. That is my sentiment as
well. All historical patterns that I have studied point
towards the inevitability of the depression of the 1990s.
But each event has a preceding cause. The new depression
is unavoidable because its seeds have already been sown
by the Reagan administration. Yet it is not too late.
Something can still be done to escape or ease the
impending crisis. True, the challenge facing us is
formidable. But where there is a will, there is a way. Where
there is no will, there are excuses!

Clearly the remedy lies in fundamental economic
reforms which go to the very root of the ills and not just
cure the symptoms. Many times before, the economy has
been in tumult which led to perfunctory changes that
merely cured the symptoms but not the cause. Never in
history have any fundamental reforms been introduced in
America. Every crisis resulted in the creation of some
institutions which solved the problem in the short run, but
created new and more serious ills in the long run. This is
how a national currency system was born in the 1860s, the
Fed in the 1910s, the New Deal in the 1930s. But problems
vanished temporarily, only to return with a crescendo.

New reforms are needed again, and let us not wait until another crisis befalls us.

Logic of Reforms

There are essentially two types of reforms—superficial and fundamental. Superficial reforms strike only at symptoms of a problem. They provide short-run cures but create side-effects which eventually make matters worse than before. However, fundamental reforms go to the heart of a malady and strike at its root cause. They essentially create a new system, stabilize it and provide a lasting cure.

Reforms that were periodically introduced in America have been superficial in nature. Let us see what such changes are bound to do. Consider Figure 1 which plots time against the horizontal axis and the evolution of any entity along the vertical axis. The diagram illustrates the time-path of any social phenomenon. According to Sarkar, motion is pulsative; nothing moves in a straight line regardless of the direction of the trend. All things evolve in cycles. When the trend is upwards, each peak is higher than the preceding peak; and when the trend is downwards, each successive trough is lower than the one before it. This is how everything behaves over time—in up and down patterns, which may be regular or irregular.

Every entity has its own momentum and a cyclical pattern of varying periodicity. At times it is in the upswing; at others, in the downswing. Let us now see what happens if some force is applied to the system from the outside.

Suppose the natural, unperturbed cycle of the entity is given by the thickly drawn pattern, AB, which has an upward trend. Suppose further that some outer force is applied at point E to reduce the depth of the downswing. Since every entity has its own internal momentum, its energy has to find an outlet in some other way. As a result, when the downswing is restrained from V to, say, D, the subsequent peak will be higher than the case would be

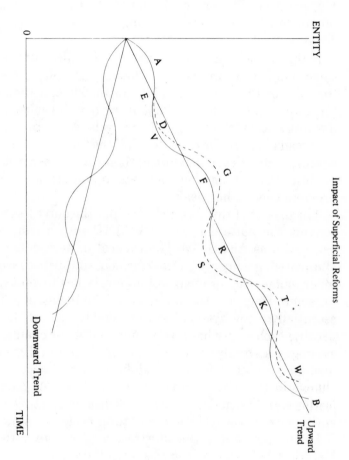

Impact of Superficial Reforms

Figure 1

155

otherwise. In other words, the effect of the outer force will be to raise the peak at point F to somewhere above it to, say, point G. The extent of the shift of F to G will be proportional to the preceding restraint over the downswing.

If the application of the outer force is discontinued at some point, then the ensuing downswing will be deeper than the one preceding it. Thus for instance, if the outer force were applied at E and not at the point of subsequent downturn, then the trough of the cycle would be at, say, S instead of R. On the other hand, if the force were applied continuously at each downturn, then the downswings will be brief and/or shallow but the upswings will be at progressively higher peaks.

The upshot of this discussion is that the outer force will convert the natural cycle AEVFRKB into a controlled cycle such as AEGSTW. The cyclical pattern cannot be eliminated; it can only be transformed, simply because the inner momentum or energy of an entity has to vent itself in some way. In the interest of enduring stability, essentially a new system has to be created out of the old, because each entity has its own momentum or energy that generates a certain type of cycle. If the natural cycle is unstable, no outer force can stabilize it for long; only a change in the natural rhythm of a system can generate lasting stability, and that means essentially creating a new entity with a relatively stable natural cycle of its own.

Let us now apply the illustration of Figure 1 to the historical behavior of the rate of inflation which had a natural cycle in 18th and 19th centuries, when the government intervention in the economy was minimal. In the upswing of the business cycle, the inflation rate would be positive; in the downswing, negative. When the Fed was established in 1914, the government began controlling the supply of money in order to eliminate or reduce the depth of the downswing. For a while this experiment was successful as there was no serious business downturn in the

1910s. But inflation of the 1910s was higher than that of any preceding decade in history. In other words, since the negative rate of inflation had been restrained by the creation of the Fed, the positive inflation rate turned out to be higher than that of any previous decade: Since the natural cycle of inflation, basically unstable, was not allowed to fully vent its energy in the business downturn, its expression had to be greater during the business upturns—a fact also substantiated by the economy's behavior since the Second World War. The cycle of inflation, as is clear from Chart 4 which is obtained from Chapter 4, reached the highest peak during the 1970s.

When another downturn came in 1929, the Fed, unlike the 1910s, failed to take any action. Hence the business downswing and the resultant negative inflation were the deepest in history, culminating in the Great Crash of the 1930s. Society learned its lessons somewhat; extensive reforms were introduced at the time to curb explosive greed of bankers and businessmen. The government also acquired counter-cyclical tools of policy recommended by Keynes. Unlike in 1929, there has been no letup in governmental interference with the economy since the 1930s. Hence business downswings and negative inflation rates have been restrained time and again, but the energy of the inflation cycle has found greater expression in its upswing. Chart 4 clearly shows that the cycle of inflation has progressively higher peaks in the 20th century than those in the 19th. The same holds true with the cycle of money growth. There again the cycle has wider fluctuations in the current century—especially after the Fed was established—than those in the previous century.

This is the point that differentiates between superficial and fundamental reforms. With superficial reforms, short-run fluctuations are curtailed, but long-run fluctuations increase. However, fundamental reforms are those that cause a lasting diminution in business oscillations. Figure 2 illustrates this case, where the natural cycle of inflation

AERB is transformed into a controlled cycle AELMC. Note that the cycle has not been eliminated; nor can it be ever, because straight-line evolution is not possible for any entity, no matter what. However, the amplitude of economic fluctuations can be reduced for a very long time with the aid of fundamental reforms. What will then happen to the inner energy of the economy? How will it then find full expression? The answer is that we will essentially be creating a new and healthier entity. Since every thing has its own rhythmical movement, the reforms have to be such that a *new* free-market economy, with a relatively stable natural cycle of its own, is created out of the current chaotic system.

Do such reforms exist? The reader has a right to be skeptical at this point. If Keynesian economics, Monetarism, Classical and Neoclassical prescriptions, and all other isms have failed to produce the long-run economic stability, is it possible to achieve it ever? Maybe such a formula just does not exist, because the best brains among the experts have not been able to discover it.

The problem is not with the lack of brains, but with the lack of motivation. Keynesians hold that capitalism is basically unstable and the government can stabilize the system; Monetarists argue that the private sector is basically stable and the government intervention causes instability. *The fact is that capitalism is fundamentally unstable, and the government's superficial action, while stabilizing it in the short run, augments its instability in the long run, when the fluctuations increase in amplitude.*

We have seen in Chapter 6 that depressions are caused primarily by extreme disparities in the distribution of wealth. This argument accords well with the law of social cycle, which states that during the age of acquisitors it is the affluent class, the prime source of inequity, that dominates society and controls its cycles.

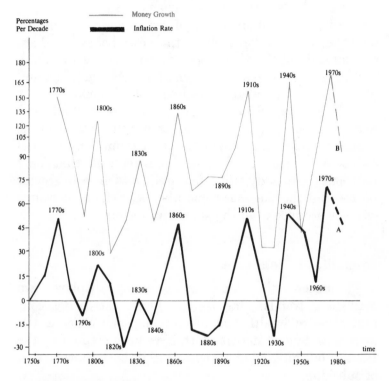

Long-Run Cycles of Inflation and Money Growth
Per Decade (1750s - 1970s)

Data sources (see the appendix)

Except for the aftermath of the Civil War of 1860s, the money-growth rate per decade reached its peak every third decade over more than two centuries, and so did the rate of inflation.

Chart 4

How Can We Prevent Another Depression?

The inner momentum or instability of capitalism springs from wealth disparities. If they are reduced, then the inherent energy of the system can be controlled and harnessed for the good of society. However, many politicians, their advisers, and their supporters are extremely affluent themselves. They can never admit that inequality is the main source of economic instability, for then they would have to blame their own behavior, or else recommend policies that work against their own interest.

Policies advocated by Keynesians, Monetarists and others strike only at the symptoms of economic ills, not at their cause, which lies in the concentration of wealth and hence of income. These policies, rather than stabilize the economy, add to its problems in the long run. Conventional economists recommend superficial reforms that only postpone the malady, which in the end returns with greater horror. But the time has come when superficial measures will not produce even the short-run results.

Immediate Measures

At present the American economy displays two disturbing trends. One is, of course, the rising concentration of wealth and income, and the other is the mammoth budget deficit. Both have been created by the massive but misguided tax cuts of 1981; both show no sign of subsiding.

An obvious way to reverse these trends is to restore the tax rates prevailing before Mr. Reagan came to office. However, this will only partially solve the problem of the budget deficit and hardly create any dent in the enormous disparity of wealth. A Federal Reserve study indicates that in 1983 people in the top 2% income bracket owned 30% of all financial assets in America [12]. Ever since the Second World War, the government has followed tax policies to reduce income and wealth inequalities, but with little success. This is because policies involving such measures

IMPACT OF FUNDAMENTAL REFORMS

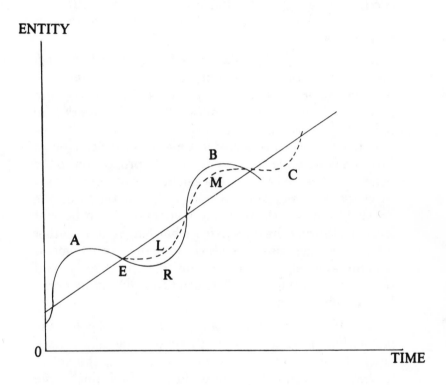

Figure 2

as the inheritance tax, progressive income tax, gift tax, etc. are riddled with so many loopholes that the affluent can easily avoid paying their full share of taxes.

Apart from removing all the escape valves, what the country needs is a *federal property tax.* Property taxes are currently levied by states and cities but not by the federal government. However, there is compelling need for such a tax today.

Much of the budget deficit is being caused by high defense spending. The purpose of strong defense presumably is to protect a person's life, liberty and property from foreign enemies. Stated differently, an individual derives three main benefits from the maintenance of armed forces. A time-honored principle of taxation is that one should pay taxes in proportion to the benefits one receives. Since life and liberty are equally dear to everybody, and since people differ in terms of the ownership of wealth, property holders ought to bear at least one third of the total defense burden. Stated another way, since defense spending provides three major benefits—namely the protection of life, liberty and property—one third of this expenditure should be borne by the owners of property.

Similar logic applies to all federal spending for the prevention of crime, because there also the benefits are much the same. In other words, one third of the entire federal expenditure for defense and the fight against crime should be borne by a federal property tax.

Certain types of properties may be exempted from this tax. Things of daily use come in this category. Thus personal residence, car, clothing, furniture, etc. qualify for the exemption. However, stocks, bonds, savings accounts, CDs, rental real estate, etc. ought to be taxed at progressive rates. And the rates should be so set that the revenue from the tax equals one third of federal spending for defense and crime control.

In 1985, the federal spending for defense and law enforcement is expected to be around $300 billion. This means that about $100 billion ought to be collected from the federal property tax. This action alone will trim the government budget deficit in half.

Benefits of the federal property tax will be considerable. Not only will it ease the problem of the budget deficit, it will also reverse the rising tide of wealth disparity. The solution of these problems in turn will postpone the great depression of 1990, and buy us time to devise and implement remedies for a lasting cure.

Another measure with great potential benefit to the U.S. and the world economy is a hefty American tariff on the import of oil, whose price rose by over 1000 percent between 1973 and 1979 and caused havoc with the international economic system. An American tariff of, say, 25% will reduce the world demand for oil, put further pressure on its already crumbling price, and could bring it down to as low as $15 per barrel. This will still be a historically high price—about five times the level in 1973.

Three major benefits will spring from this measure. First inflation will decline further; second, the tariff revenue will tend to reduce the budget deficit; and third, the international debt problem will ease, as the debtor nations on the whole are net importers of oil, and their economies will prosper as a result of the fall in the oil price.

Fundamental Economic Reforms

The federal property tax and the oil tariff will only buy us time without providing a long-term solution. For a lasting cure, we need to introduce fundamental reforms which eradicate economic as well as social ills and tensions. These reforms will create a new society with an ideal economy, which, in my view, should have the following features:

1. Its minimum wage rate satisfies a family's basic needs of food, shelter, clothing, education and medical care.

2. It provides full incentive to everyone to work hard and enjoy the fruit of his physical and intellectual labor.

3. Its inflation and unemployment rates are low but the growth rate is high.

4. It is subject to minimal oscillations around its trend, so that no one suffers undue hardship from exogenous and unforeseen shocks that periodically afflict a society.

5. Its tax system is fair and free from loopholes.

These, to me, are features of a model economy where socio-economic tensions are likely to be minimal. What kind of society can achieve this ideal?

It is clear from the outset that a totalitarian system will never attain the ideal economy, because it can never permit its citizens free choice and incentives and still retain its absolutist character. Only a free-market society is capable of reaching this goal, provided government interference is minimal. For big government draws an excessive amount of resources away from the productive private sector and leads to bureaucratic waste and inefficiency. All that the government should do is to protect the interests of the handicapped and the disadvantaged. The economic system should be such that it functions smoothly with minimum help from the state. The desirable attributes of the economy should be built into the system rather than be continually imposed from outside.

Adam Smith had demonstrated as far back as 1776 that a free-market economy enjoys maximum efficiency and high growth. However, Smith's free-enterprise system is characterized by keen competition among businessmen.

This means that wealth and income disparities among individuals cannot be too high to create monopolies, oligopolies and other forms of uncompetitive markets.

The history of Western nations, which come closest to satisfying Adam Smith's assumptions, reveals that in the long run the relatively free-market economies indeed enjoy a high degree of efficiency, growth and prosperity. However, such economies have also been convulsed time and again. This inherent tendency of Western nations can be eradicated only by minimizing wealth disparities and by creating a system where egalitarianism becomes part and parcel of the economy. The government cannot be called upon periodically to aid a crumbling structure, for in the end big government only makes matters worse. We need a system where the clamor for state intervention is the least, where unemployment compensation, food stamps, medicaid and other welfare schemes are not needed. Such a system has been devised by P.R. Sarkar, the discoverer of the social cycle, who calls it Prout, which is an acronym for Progressive (Pro), Utilization (u), Theory (t). Elsewhere I have discussed the merits and features of this system in great detail [4]. Here I present an outline of the Prout-based reforms which will give rise to a free-enterprise society that possesses attributes of the ideal economy described above:

1. Until the Proutist system is established, there should be a link between the minimum wage and the maximum wage. Specifically, the maximum salary in any industry should be no more than ten times the minimum wage.

2. Industries producing essential products and raw materials such as oil, coal, electricity, steel, should be either nationalized or divided into smaller competing units, so that monopolistic private producers cannot blackmail the entire community by withholding supplies. If

    nationalized, such industries should be managed by autonomous bodies responsible to the government on the same principles of efficiency and cost minimization as private firms facing tough competition.

3. The stock of large corporations should be distributed among blue and white collar workers, whose elected representatives should manage the industries.

4. Private initiative and investment should be limited to small corporations or proprietorships.

5. There should be ceilings on inherited wealth linked to the minimum wage.

6. The government budget should be balanced over the business cycle, that is to say, the budget should be in surplus when the economy is booming; in deficit, when the economy is in a recession.

7. Money growth should equal the average growth of the economy over the business cycle. It should be raised during recessions and reduced during booms. Yet this fine-tuning should not be carried too far.

8. Except for essential industries mentioned in the second reform, the government's intervention in the economy and society should be minimum. It should aim mainly at maintaining competition among economic agents, and promoting interests of the handicapped.

These are the fundamental economic reforms, which will eventually create the ideal economy described above. This will be an economy with a small size of government and low inequality. There will be mass capitalism or industrial democracy in which representatives of blue and white collar workers will manage industries. Profits, the main source of inequality, will be distributed among masses, and wealth disparities, once minimized through inheritance taxes, will not get a chance to return. In times of a recession, no worker will be laid off as all workers collectively manage the factories; only working hours will be reduced, so that all will equally share the burden of a business contraction. There will then be no need for unemployment compensation and the resultant bureaucracy.

Similarly, during a boom all will share the fruit of prosperity. With low wealth disparities, there will be no speculative manias and bubbles, and hence no great depressions. In short, with the aid of fundamental economic reforms, we will not only avoid the depression of 1990, but will also create an ideal economy with many desirable features.

Keynesian economics, Monetarism and others have not been able to exorcise Western society of the curse of depressions, because the reforms that they advocate strike only at the symptoms of the age-old disease. However, Prout-based reforms will eliminate the cause of the malady, and basically create a new free-market system, which will have a new natural and relatively stable rhythm of its own.

10

A General Theory of Inflation

Chapters 4 and 5 have demonstrated that inflation is not only a monetary phenomenon, it is also a regulatory phenomenon. While every peak decade of inflation in history was a peak decade of money growth, it was also a peak decade of growth in regulation. This chapter formally explains why a sustained rate of regulatory and monetary expansion generates a persistent increase in prices. In the process, we develop a simple but general theory which embodies virtually all the conventional explanations of inflation.*

The Model of Inflation

The reader has already been introduced to the concepts of aggregate demand (AD) and aggregate supply (AS). In Figure 1, these concepts are related to the general price level (P), which is an average of the prices of all goods and services. The AD line is negatively sloped to represent a negative relationship between the price level and aggregate demand. This is because as the price level rises, the purchasing power of money declines, and so does the general demand for products.

The AS line, by contrast, has a positive slope, which means that producers increase their output as the price level rises. This is because as output rises, labor productivity usually declines or wage rates increase. In either case, an increase in output is associated with a rise in labor costs per unit of production. As a result,

---

*For a more technical analysis, see R. Batra and Dan Slottje, "Money, Regulation and Inflation," SMU working paper, March, 1985.

Regulation and the Price Level

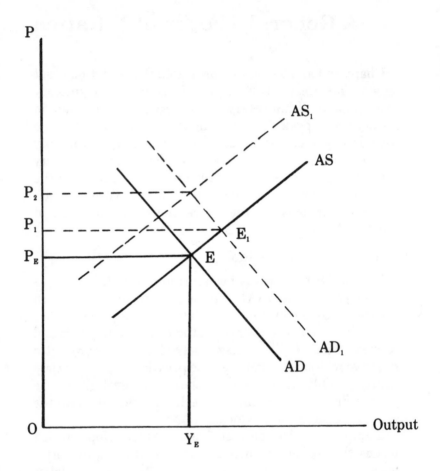

Figure 1

businessmen have to increase their prices to match the increase in their average cost. The positively sloped AS line basically reflects this idea.

The point where the two lines intersect is called the equilibrium point, where the economy eventually settles. The equilibrium output is Y_E and the equilibrium price is P_E.

Anything that shifts the AD line upwards or the AS line leftwards will cause an increase in the equilibrium price level. Suppose the AD line shifts up to AD_1, then the new equilibrium point is E_1 and the equilibrium price rises to P_1. If the AS line shifts to AS_1, the equilibrium price rises further to P_2.

Now the upward shift of the AD line is caused either by a rise in government budget deficit or by an increase in money supply, because both of them generate a rise in total spending. The AS line, however, moves leftwards whenever production cost goes up, because the firms then need a higher price to produce the same level of output. The production cost in turn rises with an exogenous rise in the wage rate, an exogenous fall in labor productivity and a rise in the price of raw materials such as oil.

Another reason for a rise in the cost of production is an increase in government regulation of business. There are costs that the firms have to incur to comply with government rules to control environmental pollution, racial and gender discrimination, product quality, etc. There are also costs involved in increased paperwork and not-so-infrequent litigation between government and the firms over the interpretation of regulatory laws. Such costs have been estimated to run into billions of dollars, and they rise with the degree of regulation. Therefore, an increase in regulation causes a rise in the price level.

The Basic Price Equation

Our analysis so far indicates that the equilibrium price level is influenced by many factors, which yield the

A General Theory of Inflation

following price equation:

$$P = aM + bD + cW - gV + fQ - hR$$

where P = price level, M = money supply, D = real government budget deficit, W = money wage rate, V = labor productivity, Q = energy price, R = degree of regulation, and where a,b,c,f,g, and h are positive numbers that measure the response of the price level to a change in the relevant variable on the right-hand side of the equation. For instance, $a = \Delta P/\Delta M$ is the response of the equilibrium price level to a change in money supply. Positive sign of "a" implies that P rises when M expands.

Let Δ indicate a change in the variable it precedes. Introducing a change in both sides of equation (1), we obtain:

$$\Delta P = a\Delta M + b\Delta D + c\Delta W - g\Delta V + f\Delta Q + h\Delta R$$

Dividing both sides of this equation by P and then dividing and multiplying each variable by itself, we obtain

$$\pi = e_M m + e_D \delta + e_W \omega - e_V \lambda + e_Q q + e_R r \qquad (2)$$

where $\pi = \Delta P/P$ is the rate of inflation, m is the rate of money growth, δ is the rate of growth of the budget deficit, ω is the rate of wage growth, λ is the rate of increase in productivity, q is the rate of increase in energy prices, r is the rate of growth in regulation, and the various e's, all defined to be positive, are the elasticities of P with respect to the respective variable. Thus $e_M = (\Delta P/P \div \Delta M/M) = (\Delta P/\Delta M \div M/P) = aM/P$ is the elasticity of the price level with respect to money supply and so on.

Equation (2) states that inflation accelerates with a rise in money growth, deficit growth, wage growth, energy price inflation and regulatory growth, but falls with an increase in the growth of productivity. Although this equation furnishes various determinants of the rate of inflation, its relation with popular explanations is not yet complete.

Since the government must finance its deficit either by issuing bonds or through money creation,

$$PD = \Delta M + \Delta B = (M - M_{-1}) + (B - B_{-1}) \qquad (3)$$

where B is the nominal value of government bonds. Equation (3) says that nominal government deficit in the current period is financed either by new money creation, equaling the difference between money supply in the current period and that in the previous period (M_{-1}), or by the sale of new government bonds, equaling $\Delta B = B - B_{-1}$. Since the last period's values are given, introducing change in both sides of equation (3) yields:

$$D\Delta P + P\Delta D = \Delta M + \Delta B$$

Dividing both sides by PD, we have:

$$\pi + \delta = \alpha_M m + \alpha_B b \qquad (4)$$

where $\alpha_M = M/PD$ is the money to deficit ratio, $\alpha_B = B/PD$ is the debt to deficit ratio and $b = \Delta B/B$ is the rate of growth of nominal debt.

What is the difference between the growth rate of money present in equation (2) and that in equation (4)? In (2), m is money growth representing some monetary policy, whereas in (4) m is money growth caused by expansionary fiscal policy. The two ought to be combined to obtain the full impact of money growth on inflation. This we do in a short while.

A popular explanation of inflation is provided by what is known as the Phillip's curve, which in its recent form says that

$$\omega = \pi_e + \frac{\omega_0}{U}, \qquad\qquad \omega_0 > 0$$

A General Theory of Inflation

and

$$U = h\frac{\overline{Y}-Y}{\overline{Y}} = hz$$

so that

$$\omega = \pi_e + \frac{\omega_0}{hz} = \pi_e + \frac{\omega_1}{z}, \tag{5}$$

where U = rate of unemployment, π_e = expected rate of inflation, $\overline{Y}$ = full employment level of output, $\omega_1 = \omega_0/h$ and $z = (\overline{Y} - Y)/\overline{Y}$ is a measure of the GNP gap in the economy. According to equation (5), the rate of increase in the money wage is a positive function of the expected rate of inflation and a negative function of the GNP gap, which, in view of Okun's law, is proportional to unemployment. Equation (5) is the well-known expectations-augmented Phillip's curve.

Substituting equations (4) and (5) in (2), we obtain:

$$\pi = \frac{1}{1+e_D}\left[(e_M + \alpha_M e_D)m + \alpha_B e_D b + e_w(\pi_e + \omega_1/z)\right.$$
$$\left. -e_V\lambda + e_Q q + e_R r\right] \tag{6}$$

Equation (6) is a reduced form equation which says that inflation is a positive function of money growth, nominal debt growth, expected inflation rate, energy price increase, regulatory growth, and a negative function of the GNP gap and the rate of growth of productivity. It is developed from the standard AD-AS model, but it captures many popular explanations of inflation. Thus, Friedman's monetarism is captured by the positive coefficient of m; the Phillip's curve explanation is captured by the positive coefficient of $1/z$; another hypothesis, called the productivity slow-down theory, finds expression in the negative coefficient of λ; the

Keynesian fiscalist explanation is displayed by the positive coefficient of b; the energy-price explanation is represented by the positive value of e_Q; the inflationary expectations hypothesis is expressed by the positive coefficient of π_e, and, above all, the effect of the growth in regulation is captured by the positive coefficient of r.

Inflation in the Long Run

Equation (6) is the fundamental equation of inflation. It captures virtually all the popular explanations of inflation. However, in the long run only those variables matter which are truly exogenous and hence independent of the market forces of demand and supply. A rise in wages, or energy prices or a fall in productivity usually have one-shot effect on the price level. For a sustained increase in the price level, the determining variables must rise for a long time. Since wages and energy prices are subject to market forces and are not independent of the level of GNP, they cannot increase constantly over the long run. Similarly, productivity also usually stops declining after a while.

The variables which can maintain sustained growth for some time are usually independent of economic conditions. Quite often they are dictated by politics. Thus, the growth of money, debt, and regulation is subject to political forces, and in the long run only these three variables are the true determinants of inflation.

Empirical Evidence

Before we estimate the long-run version of equation (6), it is necessary to specify a function for expected inflation. Recent empirical work by Meltzer* suggests that inflationary expectations are determined mainly by sustained rates of monetary expansion. Meltzer obtains his expected inflation variable by regressing the actual inflation rate against current and three years' average money growth.

---

*Meltzer, L., "Anticipated Inflation and Unanticipated Price Change," *Journal of Money, Credit and Banking*, June 1977.

A General Theory of Inflation

In our study based on long-run data, sustained monetary expansion can be readily identified with the decennial rate of money growth. The Meltzer expectations hypothesis is that

$$\pi_e = \hat{a}_0 + \hat{a}_1 m, \quad \hat{a}_1 > 0$$

where $\hat{a}_0$ and $\hat{a}_1$ are the coefficients estimated by regressing observed inflation rates against sustained money growth. This hypothesis, however, implies that agents completely ignore current information about actual inflation rates in forming future expectations. A more general expectations hypothesis is presented in (7):

$$\pi_e = b_0 + b_1 x + b_2 x^2, \quad b_1 > 0, \quad b_2 < 0 \qquad (7)$$

where $x = m/\pi$ is the ratio of money growth and the rate of inflation. Equation (7) suggests that if rational agents find that money growth has been rising faster than the observed rate of inflation for some time, they expect inflation to rise in the future, and conversely. The negative coefficient of x^2 implies that as x rises, π_e rises but at a decreasing rate, so that π_e has an upper bound.

In what follows, we follow the estimation procedure used by Meltzer. That is, we first estimate the expected rate of inflation and then use these estimates to obtain the equation for the actual rate of inflation.

Before concluding this section, it is perhaps necessary to examine the desirability of using decennial data for purposes of estimation. Even though Kuznets used this procedure extensively, such data are hardly ever used in regression analysis. There are pros and cons to this empirical approach. The cons are that it ignores the short-term fluctuations occuring during a decade. My response is that this sort of work already abounds, whereas regression analysis of inflation in terms of the decade-to-decade data, to my knowledge, has not been conducted before. And this approach yields many surprises, of which some have been reported in earlier chapters.

The time period covered by our estimation is 1800-1980. This is because data for federal debt, available from [33] and [34], goes only back to 1800. Other data is available from Table 1, Chapter 3 and Table 3, Chapter 5. The first step in the regression analysis is to obtain an equation for expected inflation, which we estimate by regressing actual inflation against x, the ratio of money growth and inflation. This equation, using ordinary least squares, is:

$$\pi_e = \hat{\pi} = 7.45 + 3.7x - 0.45x^2$$
$$\quad\quad (1.15)\ (2.53)\ (-2.57)$$

where the "t" statistics are in the parenthesis. Both x and x^2 are significant at 5% level, as the 't' value for each exceeds two.

Using $\hat{\pi}$ for expected inflation, we regress actual inflation against money growth, debt growth and the degree of regulation, and obtain the following equation while using the Cochrun-Orcutt procedure:

$$\pi_t = -49.1 + 0.36m_t + 0.15m_{t-1} - 0.001b_t$$
$$\quad\quad (-4.7)\quad (3.6)\quad\quad (1.7)\quad\quad (-1.1)$$

$$+\ 0.86\pi_{et} + 0.36r_t ;$$
$$\quad (3.5)\quad\quad (2.9)$$

$$R^2 = 0.8,\ \bar{R}^2 = 0.7,\ F_{(5,12)} = 9.3$$

As seen earlier in Chapter 4, money growth is the primary determinant of inflation, but its effects last over two decades. Here m_t has a positive and highly significant coefficient, and m_{t-1} has a smaller but still somewhat significant effect. A 1% rise in money growth in a decade raises the inflation rate by .36% in that decade and by .15% in the next decade. Thus the cumulative effect of money growth on inflation is very high.

In addition to money growth, expected inflation and regulatory growth are also significant determinants of inflation, whereas the growth of debt exerts no influence. Since expected inflation is itself determined by money growth, the regression analysis confirms, what we have already concluded in Chapters 4 and 5, that inflation is a monetary as well as a regulatory phenomenon.

11

Macroeconomic
Thought: A Synthesis

Macroeconomics, at this juncture, is suffering from a great deal of confusion. At last count, excluding the Socialists and Radicals, there were eight major schools of thought—Classicists, Neoclassicists, Keynesians, Post-Keynesians, Neo-Keynesians, Monetarists, Rational Expectationists, and Supply-Siders. All these schools diverge from each other, some radically, some only a shade. They all examine the economic behavior of society as a whole, offering a spectrum of policy prescriptions.

A closer study, however, reveals that all these viewpoints fall in two categories. In reality, there are only two main schools of thought, namely the interventionist school, and the non-interventionist school: The two generic ideas encompass all macroeconomic philosophies.

According to the interventionist school, government should periodically fine-tune the economy with the aid of its monetary and fiscal policies. The private sector on its own is unstable, but the state can stabilize it by intervening in its financial institutions such as bond and money markets. During a recession the treasury ought to use the bond market to borrow money from the public so as to finance the budget deficit, and the Fed should purchase securities to help banks expand the supply of money. Such are the intervening methods of the interventionist school, which includes Keynesians, Post-Keynesians and Neo-Keynesians. The three may differ on the emphasis to be given to the various interfering tools, but on the question of state intervention, they all concur.

Macroeconomic Thought: A Synthesis

The non-interventionist school, comprising the remaining viewpoints, detests the idea of economic fine-tuning by the state on logical as well as ideological grounds. Government, in its view, ought to keep its hands off the economy or adhere to rigid rules regarding money growth and balancing of the federal budget. The private sector on its own is efficient and stable, but government interference destabilizes it and makes it inefficient. The state aid may offer short-term palliatives, but it cannot offer a long-term cure.

These then are the two broad viewpoints in which all the popular schools of macroeconomics can be classified. Where does the law of social cycle come in? Where do Sarkar's views fit in this configuration?

The law of social cycle is a vast synthesis, an all-inclusive hypothesis in harmony with divergent ideas prevalent not only in economics but also in many other disciplines. In this theory there is no dogmatic acceptance or rejection of one view to the exclusion of all others. It explains when and why certain philosophies emerge and capture popular attention.

In the first half of the age of acquisitors, non-interventionist views develop and become the accepted doctrine. As the power and prestige of the opulent grow, government is decentralized and the ideas of individualism replace those of state-collectivism. It is only in a decentralized setting that wealth can play a strong political role. Being scattered across the nation, the affluent can exert influence only when the central authority is weak. Therefore only individualistic, rather than statist, doctrines are acceptable to the wealthy class.

A decentralized government such as a democracy or a feudalistic regime constitutes one aspect of individualism. Another aspect is *laissez-faire*, that is, the state should not intervene in the economy or in the economic liberty and rights of the individuals. Thus, the reason why the Classical theology of *laissez-faire* became so popular during 18th and 19th centuries is that the wealthy were not only then the dominant class, the age of acquisitors in America was also then in its rising phase. There was hardly any opposition to the supremacy of the opulent at that time.

In every age of acquisitors, individualistic ideas gradually give way to statist ideas, which call for state intervention in societal affairs in the interest of social welfare. In fact, the rise of interventionist attitudes, which pose a challenge to the undisputed primacy of the affluent class, signifies that the acquisitive era is in its declining phase.

Whenever the dominant class is in trouble, it seeks guidance from the intellectuals, who by nature like to devise numerous rules and regulations to solve any problem. Intellectuals as a class generally offer that advice which requires interference in individual and family affairs. Thus, during the downturn of the age of acquisitors, who turn to intellectuals because of mounting economic ills, interventionist philosophies become popular in society. That is precisely why, following the massive economic collapse during the 1930s when the government controlled by the wealthy turned to experts for advice, the interventionist viewpoint of Keynes became the accepted doctrine.

The crux of this discussion is that individualistic, non-interventionist theories become prominent in the first half or the upswing of the age of acquisitors. However, during the second half of the acquisitive era, interventionist viewpoints gradually become dominant, and in the final stages, there is a muddle of economic doctrines, offering a confusing picture. This is what happened during feudalism, and the same type of evolution has been occurring during capitalism, which is the West's modern age of acquisitors.

The Classical and Neoclassical theories of individualism were prevalent during the 19th century, because that was the first half of the modern era of acquisitors. Since the 1930s, however, the Keynesian interventionist philosophy has reigned supreme and other ideas have merely provided it a challenge with mediocre success. Monetarism, Rational Expectations, and the Supply-Side cures are all modern but refined versions of the Classical economic ideology which, at least in the matter of practical policy, has failed to dethrone the Keynesian orthodoxy. The Keynesian prescription of high budget deficit to combat unemployment has been followed by virtually all U.S. Presidents, beginning with John F. Kennedy in 1961.

Sarkar's hypothesis is not dogmatic; far from it. Keynesian and Monetarist ideas are but little buds in the all-comprehensive bouquet of social cycle. To Friedman, money is the primary determinant of all economic activity. Sarkar goes a step further and argues that wealth including money is the primary determinant of not only the economic activity but of all predominant institutions during the era of acquisitors. Monetarism is thus a special little case of the law of social cycle.

For years Keynesians and Monetarists have been locked in a debate over the importance of money in economic activity. Chapters 3, 4, and 5 have established beyond a shadow of doubt that Monetarists have been right after all. These chapters also offer convincing support to Sarkar's theory that during the age of the wealthy, of which capitalism is but one facet, wealth or money is the prime mover of social phenomena.

We have seen earlier that the regular cycles of money growth, inflation and regulation have all crested together in the United States. The question is: Which is the dominant cycle among them?

As regards inflation, money growth is clearly the determining variable. It is true that inflation itself may cause a rise in money supply. In fact, this is what generates the cycle. First, money supply grows for a long time, leading to the emergence of inflation, which in turn raises money demand, thereby generating further growth in money. Eventually, the public is fed up and demands actions from politicians. They respond by restraining the engine of money supply, thus putting an end to the spiral of inflation. Clearly, then the cycle of money growth dictates the cycle of inflation.

In a free-enterprise system, prices determine all economic activity. Inflation is nothing but a change in prices. Thus, the cycle of money growth, by controlling the cycle of price changes, must eventually control the cycles in economic activity. In the long run, there can be no other way, although in the short run, a la Keynes, economic activity may not respond predictably and significantly to variations in money supply.

The cycle of money growth dominates economic activity in yet another way -- through its impact on regulation. No one doubts that federal regulation significantly affects economic as well as societal activity. We have seen before that the cycles of money growth and regulation are virtually parallel to each other. This is the best proof of Sarkar's dictum that during the era of the affluent, where money is the main source of political power, wealth is the primary determinant of not only economic activity but of all major institutions in society.

One may argue that it is the cycle of regulation that governs the cycle of money growth, and not vice-versa. If this is true, then intellectuals, not the acquisitors, have been running the levers of U.S. society.

There is no doubt that intellectuals as a class have been quite influential in American history. But they have usually, if not always, served the interests of the affluent, and occasionally enriched themselves. This is true even after the rise of the pro- interventionist sentiment among economists. State policies have generally furthered the concerns of big business-- at least in practice, though perhaps not always in theory. Thus, the affluent, not intellectuals, have determined the course of American society in its history.

One may also argue that money and wealth are not totally identical, as money is only a fraction of wealth which also includes stocks, bonds, real estate, jewelry, cars, etc. Nor is the growth of money the same thing as the growth of wealth. Money supply may expand but wealth may stagnate or even decline, if real economic activity fails to respond to monetary expansion.

These are all valid points. Money supply is at best a proxy for wealth. Ideally, we would like to have continuous data on the growth of wealth and examine its behavior over time. But since such data is unavailable, money growth is the next best thing we can analyze. In any case, money is commonly used as a wealth variable in macroeconomics.

Throughout U.S. history, the top one percent families have owned 20% to 36% of tangible national wealth. They have also owned over a quarter of aggregate money balances. With the cycle of money growth dictating the cycles of inflation and regulation, it is now crystal clear that it is the top one percent owners of wealth who have been the architects of socio-economic phenomena all through the U.S. chronicle.

This is Sarkar's Monetarism, of which Friedman's Monetarism is a special case. Since we have established the validity of Sarkar's version, Friedman's version automatically holds.

After all this is said, what precisely is the role of ideas offered by Keynes? In terms of Sarkar's thesis, Keynesian economics and its offshoots provide the dividing line separating the first period of the acquisitive era from its second period. The influence of acquisitors was in its upswing when Classical economics was popular. Their influence moved into its downswing with the onset of Keynesian revolution, although the affluent continued to be the dominant voice in society. Thus Keynesian economics also finds its niche in the historical setting of the law of social cycle.

What about the remedies offered by Keynes? In Sarkar's view, such measures only cure the symptoms without treating the cause of economic and hence social instability.

They do provide relief in the short run but worsen the malady in the long run. The Classical prescriptions of state inactivism are also of little help, because they resulted in cataclysmic depressions in the past. Is there no hope for society then? There is! The hope lies in fundamental economic reform sketched out in Chapter 9.

Sarkar's law of social cycle is thus a vast synthesis in which all schools of macroeconomic thought, however divergent, have a place. Indeed, all visions of society have a place in it.

REFERENCES

1. Batra, R., *Capitalism and Communism: A New Study of History*, London: Macmillan, 1978.
2. _____, "The Long-Run Cycles of Money Growth and Inflation in the United States," *Renaissance Universal Journal*, Vol. 2-3, 1984.
3. _____, *Muslim Civilization and the Crisis in Iran*, Venus Books, Dallas, 1980.
4. _____, *Prout*, University Press of America, Lanham, 1980.
5. Beard, C.A. and M.R., *The Rise of American Civilization*, Vol. I. Macmillan, New York, 1925.
6. Brunner, K., *The Great Depression Revisited*, Martinus Nijhoff, New York, 1981.
7. Bureau of the Budget, *The United States at War*, 1947.
8. Burns, E.M. and P.L. Ralph, *World Civilizations*, W.W. Norton, New York, 1974.
9. Clark, L.H. and A.L. Malabre, "Economists Don't See Threats to Economy Portending Depression," *Wall Street Journal*, October 12, 1984.
10. _____, and L. McGinley, "Monetarists Succeed in Pushing Basic Ideas But not Their Policies," *Wall Street Journal*, December 10, 1984.
11. Dornbusch, R. and S. Fischer, *Macroeconomics*, 3rd. ed., McGraw Hill, New York, 1983.
12. Federal Reserve Board, "Survey of Consumer Finances, 1983," *Federal Reserve Bulletin*, September 1984.
13. Fite, G.C. and J.E. Reese, *An Economic History of the United States*, Houghton Mifflin, Boston, 1973.

14. Friedman, M., *Capitalism and Freedom*, University of Chicago Press, Chicago, 1962.
15. Friedman, M. and A. Schwartz, *A Monetary History of the United States, 1867-1960*, Princeton University Press, 1963.
16. Gallman, R.E., "Trends in the Size Distribution of Wealth in the Nineteenth Century," in *Six Papers on the Size Distribution of Wealth and Income*, ed. Lee Soltow, NBER, New York, 1969.
17. Gurley, J.G. and E.S. Shaw, "The Growth of Debt and Money in the United States," *Review of Economics and Statistics*, August 1957, p. 258.
18. Heeth, Bob, "Economics Expert Predicts Spread of War," *Nashville Banner*, September 30, 1980.
19. Kindleberger, C.P., *Manias, Panics and Crashes*, Basic Books, New York, 1978.
20. Lacroix, Paul, *History of Prostitution*, Covici, Friede, New York, 1931.
21. Lampman, R.J., *The Share of Top Wealthholders in National Income*, NBER, New York, 1962.
22. McElvaine, R.S., *The Great Depression: America 1929-1941*, Times Books, New York, 1984.
23. Penoyer, R., *Directory of Regulatory Agencies*, Center for the Study of American Business, Washington University, St. Louis, 1981 and 1982.
24. Primack, M.L. and J. Willis, *An Economic History of the United States*, Benjamin Cummings, Menlo Park, 1980.
25. Saint-Etienne, C., *The Great Depression, 1929-38*: The Lesson for the 1980s, Hoover Institution Press, California, 1984.
26. Sarkar, P.R., *Human Society, II*, A.M. Press, Denver, 1967.

27. Schnitzer, M., *Contemporary Government and Business Relations*, Houghton Mifflin, Boston, 1983.
28. Smith, J.D. and S.D. Franklin, "The Concentration of Personal Wealth, 1922-1969," *American Economic Review*, May 1974, 162-67.
29. Soltow, Lee, *Men and Wealth in the United States, 1850-1870*, Yale University Press, New Haven, 1975.
30. Temin, Peter, *Did Monetary Forces Cause the Great Depression?*, Norton, New York, 1976.
31. *The Tennessean*, "Prof Catches People's Attention with Predictions," October 14, 1980.
32. Turner, J.H. and C.E. Starnes, *Inequality: Privilege and Poverty in America*, Goodyear Publishing Company, Pacific Palisades, 1976.
33. U.S. Department of Commerce, *Historical Statistics of the United States*, 1975.
34. U.S. Printing Office, *Economic Report of the President*, 1983.
35. Volcker, Paul, *The Rediscovery of the Business Cycle*, Free Press, New York, 1978.
36. Williamson, J.G. and P.H. Lindert, *American Inequality: A Macroeconomic History*, Academic Press, New York, 1980.
37. Willoughby, W.F., *Government Organization in War Time and After*, Macmillan, London, 1919.
38. Winter, R., "A Low Inflation Rate Can Be Painful," *Wall Street Journal*, December 11, 1984.

INDEX

190